YOUTH **LIFESTYLES**
IN A CHANGING WORLD

YOUTH **LIFESTYLES**
IN A CHANGING WORLD

Steven Miles

OPEN UNIVERSITY PRESS
Buckingham · Philadelphia

Open University Press
Celtic Court
22 Ballmoor
Buckingham
MK18 1XW

email: enquiries@openup.co.uk
world wide web: http://www.openup.co.uk

and
325 Chestnut Street
Philadelphia, PA 19106, USA

First Published 2000

ISBN   0 335 20098 2 (pb)   0 335 20099 0 (hb)

A catalogue record of this book is available from the British Library

Library of Congress Cataloging-in-Publication Data
Miles, Steven.
    Youth lifestyles in a changing world/Steven Miles.
       p. cm.
    Includes bibliographical references and index.
    ISBN 0-335-20098-2 (pbk.) – ISBN 0-335-20099-0 (hb)
    1. Youth – Social conditions. 2. Young consumers. 3 Lifestyles. 4. Social
change. I. Title
HQ796.M4783 2000
305.235–dc21   99-056818

Copy-edited and typeset by The Running Head Limited,
www.therunninghead.com
Printed in Great Britain by Biddles Ltd, Guildford and King's Lynn

To Phoebe

CONTENTS

PREFACE

This book is about the changing nature of young people's lives at the beginning of the twenty-first century. The book came about as part of a recognition that the sociology of youth appears to have struggled to come to terms with what it means to be a young person in a changing world. Young people appear to be at the 'cutting edge' of social and cultural change and yet the sociology of youth has failed to cope with the complexities that these changes have engendered. The paradoxes that young people have to cope with on a day-to-day basis are immense. The suggestion explored in *Youth Lifestyles in a Changing World* is that young people's lifestyles represent a key arena within which young people confront such paradoxes. The term 'youth' is a highly contested one. Young people's experiences are arguably so diverse that it has almost become meaningless to categorize young people in this fashion. This book will suggest, however, that young people *do* call upon their lifestyles as a common resource, a breathing space within which they can actively, and at times creatively, cope with the constant uncertainties apparently characteristic of life in a so-called 'post-modern' world.

The initial idea for this book emerged out of a piece of research I conducted on consumer lifestyles and identities that I began while working at the University of Huddersfield. I thank the young people I interviewed as well as my friends and colleagues at Huddersfield for putting me on the right track. More recently, a special thanks to all my colleagues in the Department of Sociology at the University of Plymouth for their part in creating such a supportive environment in which to work. I would also like to thank LK for her efforts in a phone box in Dover. A final word of thanks to Justin Vaughan, Viv Cracknell and everybody at Open University Press and The Running Head who helped bring this book to life.

Youth Lifestyles in a Changing World is intended to encourage students, researchers and academics alike to reflect on how the world around them is changing and how such changes might affect what it currently means to be a 'young' person. Writing this book may not have made me any younger, but it has hopefully provided a springboard from which both the reader and I can take stock of both our own role and sociology's role in an ever-changing world.

1
CONCEPTUALIZING 'YOUTH'

For too long social scientists have portrayed young people as excluded risk-taking trouble-makers motivated by nothing more than their own rebellious self-interest. The everyday realities of young people's lifestyles as an expression or reproduction of the dominant values of society have, in turn, too often been neglected. Young people are not always rebellious and are not simply on a mission to undermine society or that society as it appears to be represented to them by their parents. Nor is it possible or even desirable to generalize about what it is that constitutes 'youth', because youth is far more complicated than a single word inevitably implies. In fact, young people's experiences are eminently diverse and will be differentiated, among other things, according to variations in class, gender and education. The contention here, however, is that it is still possible to identify some key characteristics of young people's experiences which have a powerful and widespread influence on both the construction of their everyday lives and their identities. Angela McRobbie (1993) points out that youth represents a major symbolic investment for society as a whole and for this reason the richness of young people's experience needs to be addressed in a far more sophisticated manner than is currently the case. *Youth Lifestyles in a Changing World* will therefore seek to redress some of the over-romanticized, media-generated, and quite often misguided conceptions of youth that have dominated sociological thought in the past thirty or forty years, and by doing so will monitor the diversities, commonalities and experiences which characterize young people's life-styles today.

The sociological study of youth is fascinating not only because it has the potential to tell us so much about what it means to be a young person in contemporary society, but because it can also tell us so much about the changing nature of social life in general. In this context, McRobbie (1993) suggests that young people are constantly making 'statements' of one form or another and that these statements take different shapes under different historical conditions and yet continue to be made. The key question is therefore: what statements are young people currently making and why? Young people represent a rich source of sociological debate and discussion, but the trick lies in pursuing such discussions down avenues that accurately reflect young people's experiences of social change:

> Perhaps by examining these changes, by investigating the processes that affect both young people and adults, we can identify a common ground of experience which can be discussed despite the differences in our languages, points of view, ages, and roles. Young people are the primary subjects of dramatic transformations that affect contemporary society and experience them most directly. Parents, teachers, and adults can learn about themselves by listening to youngsters.
> (Melucci 1992: 52)

The intention of this book is therefore to construct a grounded and critically aware discussion of youth lifestyles in a changing world. Above all, the priority here is to actively address the suggestion made by authors such as Hollands (1995) and Williamson (1997a) that young people need to be provided with a voice which actually addresses what it means to be part of the sorts of social changes that they experience daily. How, in effect, do young people interact with and negotiate the social worlds in which they construct their everyday lives? In this chapter I will introduce some of the problems sociologists have encountered in their attempt to come to terms with the nature of the relationship between young people and social change. In particular, I will highlight the tensions caused by the division that exists in the sociology of youth between structural and cultural approaches to young people's changing lives.

Young people and social change

Many authors have pointed out that young people are a barometer of social change. In addition, Jones and Wallace (1992) note that young people might equally be conceptualized as an index of social *ills*. This latter proposition may well be the case, but there is also a strong argument for suggesting that by accentuating an image of young people simply as a social group likely to feel the full force of society's more negative aspects such as unemployment, drug misuse and teenage pregnancy, the actual intricacies of young people's experiences have been misunderstood. Not all young people are submerged in the melodrama of subcultural life or the terrors of drug addiction and alcohol consumption. In many ways young people are an index of social *norms*. But for too long sociology has neglected what I will describe as 'mainstream youth' in favour of a sociology of the melodramatic and perhaps more worryingly of the 'problematic', which as a result has underestimated the degree of complexity that characterizes young people's lives.

As Osgerby (1998a) notes, far from being an immutably fixed and timeless stage in human physical and psychological development, the nature of youth varies enormously across time and cultures. The contention underlying this book as a whole is that social change is such that traditional forms of transition into adulthood have been increasingly undermined, in the sense that adult roles are less easily assumed or assimilated (see Hollands 1995). Indeed, what is perhaps most interesting about youth at the start of a new millennium is that the youth experience is as varied now as it ever has been in history and yet, paradoxically, young people continue to be bonded by common experiences and concerns. Sociologists have traditionally tended to focus on extreme cultural expressions of youth at one end of the spectrum and conceptions of 'disadvantaged' youth at the other. On this basis there has been a tendency to extract meaning from either melodramatic expressions of lifestyle or from structural conceptions of youth disadvantage as a basis for further generalizations about the nature of youth as a whole.

Cultural conceptions of youth

As Thornton (1997) points out, one of the main problems with cultural approaches to the sociology of youth is that they have tended to focus on the subordinacy of youth. Research has often focused on youth subcultures which have been perceived to be deviant or debased, but also low down the social ladder due to exclusionary experiences based on class, race, ethnicity and age (Thornton 1997: 4). Although sociologists and subcultural researchers have, in effect, used youth as a vehicle for the systematic study of the cultural (which in itself is a more than worthwhile exercise), by doing so they have labelled and therefore framed, shaped and delineated social formations. This has resulted in the relationship between the subordinate and the dominant culture (and those that might actively abide by that culture) becoming increasingly blurred. In this context, authors such as Wyn and White (1997) have noted how the tendency to categorize young people, as if age represents the central feature characterizing their lives, has tended to portray masculine, white (and rebellious) middle-class experience as the norm. In this context

> A categorical approach also ignores the significant role of institutions and of changing economic and political circumstances and their impact on youth. The result is the tendency to present the attitudes, behaviours and styles of particular groups as normative and to underestimate diversity amongst young people.
>
> (Wyn and White 1997: 13)

Perhaps the classic example of work of this type, which in hindsight can be criticized for the above limitations, is that undertaken by the Centre for Contemporary Cultural Studies in Birmingham in the 1970s (see Epstein 1998 for a detailed discussion). Basing its conception of young people very much upon what it is to be deviant, the Birmingham School argue that young people establish who it is they are through a process of labelling. By combining the insights of symbolic interactionism, structural functionalism and semiology, the Birmingham School tried to move away from mass media portrayals of spectacular youth cultures in order to establish a more grounded, realistic and objective portrayal of young people's lives which were seen to be resistant to hegemonic cultural forms. In other words, the Birmingham School was concerned with the ways in which the young expressed themselves in opposition to a culture in which their voice was rarely heard.

Subcultural styles incorporate the recontextualization of objects to communicate fresh meanings via bricolage or pastiche (Epstein 1998: 13). In this context, perhaps of most relevance to this book is Dick Hebdige's (1979) *Subculture: The Meaning of Style*. Lying at the core of Hebdige's argument is the suggestion that young people express their resistance to authority through visual styles. He argues that youth subcultures represent a form of genuinely expressive subterranean style and, 'a symbolic violation of the social order' (p. 19). Interestingly, Hebdige sees the increase in spending power among working-class youth during the 1970s and the creation of a market to absorb the resulting surplus as having a key role in the changing nature of youth lifestyles. However, Hebdige and the Birmingham School in general are often criticized for the way in which they deploy a Marxist delinquency-based theoretical framework 'whilst denying deviant groups a radical effectivity by arguing that bourgeois society utilises the new mass institutions to its own ends. Subcultures then simply become rituals acted out within a class structure' (Stratton 1985: 204).

In turn, there may well be a strong argument to suggest that despite providing the sociology of youth with a considerable legacy (for reasons which I will consider throughout this book), this sort of deviancy model is in fact becoming less relevant to what it is to be a young person at the beginning of the twenty-first century. There may well be a case for arguing, as does Cohen (1980), that the latent function of subcultures is to somehow magically solve – even if in little more than an imaginary way – the unresolved contradictions of the parent culture. But what should be of more importance here is not the good intentions behind subcultural forms. Of potentially more interest is the suggestion that despite all their gesturing and all their achievements in constructing a sense of group identity, young people's efforts are arguably redundant in the sense that they can ultimately do little more than prop up dominant power structures.

It would be misleading to suggest that the sociology of youth culture is still dependent upon Birmingham-style subcultural analyses, but its influence is clearly still in evidence. It is also fair to say that disaffection with the term 'subculture' has become increasingly prevalent in Britain. Sadly, however, this is as a reflection of what Redhead (1997: 3) describes as 'the virtual disappearance of a "field" of "appreciative" contemporary sociological and cultural studies of youth culture'. In effect, the sociology of cultural aspects of young people's lives has appeared to have lost its impetus since the 1980s, arguably because there are simply fewer 'committed' youths upon which sociologists can focus their subcultural attention in a world where 'ordinary' youths are the norm. Those studies that do exist tend to pursue a theoretical vacuum in which the cultural contexts in which young people operate are rarely related to the sorts of social pressures they are experiencing. In this context, the over-emphasis on rave cultures as being representative of more general youth experience has been especially damaging, as I will point out in Chapter 6.

The development of youth subcultures as a focus for sociological research has been interesting in a broader sense in so far as the emergence of this area of study has reflected an associated struggle to come to terms with appropriate conceptual tools. Hence, the sociology of youth is riddled with highly contested notions such as 'transition', 'youth culture' and 'subculture'. The notion of youth 'subculture' is worthy of particular attention as it has played such an instrumental role in the development of the sociology of youth throughout the 1970s and 1980s.

A more detailed critique of the continued sociological significance of youth subcultures should provide a context within which we can begin to consider the nature of youth lifestyles which, I will argue, represent a potentially more enlightening means of coming to terms with young people's relationship with social change. One of the most insightful recent discussions of the development of subcultures as a focus for socio- logical research can be found in the work of Widdicombe and Wooffitt (1995) who argue that the notion of subculture has been prioritized by sociologists precisely because it represents the most *visible* aspect of the youth experience. In effect, the way in which youth subcultures have been too readily identified as an indicator of social change (and in particular of social ills) has meant that they 'have been given signi- ficance and prominence within much broader sociological debates, and beyond the lives of the minority of adolescents who are involved' (Widdicombe and Wooffitt 1995: 7). More specifically, Widdicombe and Wooffitt argue that sociologists have been too theoretical in their treat- ment of youth subcultures and have failed to accommodate actors' own accounts or experiences. This might well be because the methods that sociologists traditionally used to understand youth subcultures were bound up with notions of class and resistance. The process of com- modification appears to have undermined this analysis in the sense that the oppositional force constituted by young people has arguably been incorporated into the dominant order. Subculture, in effect, has arguably been commodified and 'made palatable for popular consumption' (McRobbie 1993: 411).

But, just because sociologists have tended to misuse the notion of 'youth subcultures', this does not mean that we should dismiss it entirely as a conceptual tool. Indeed, as Widdicombe and Wooffitt (1995) them- selves point out, used appropriately it still has much to offer analyti- cally. Youth subcultures can be said to offer young people a sense of identity different from that which is ascribed for them by school, work and class. Style, lifestyle, image, values and ideology therefore provide the symbolic resources through which identities can be constructed: 'This in turn enables individuals to escape effectively their ascribed iden- tities, and therefore (psychologically at least) to escape the problems which the ascribed categories entail' (Widdicombe and Wooffitt 1995: 24). In effect then, youth subcultures give young people the opportunity to experience a sense of social reality independent of the adult world which they inhabit; they provide the space within which young people can be young people. It is easy to forget, however, that young people's cultural lives actively reflect their relationship to dominant power structures. This book will suggest that the nature of such structures and their cultural expression have changed to such an extent that nowadays the notion of youth *lifestyles* is now potentially far more useful than that of youth subcultures.

The danger with a subcultural approach to youth is that subcultural analyses of young people's experience, as I imply above, simplify what being a young person is all about and, by doing so, focus on specific spaces in which young people can be themselves at the expense of many other such spaces. More often than not, this has tended to involve the media portraying young people as harbingers of moral panic to the extent that the creative possibilities and the real problems experienced by young people are neglected (see Hollands 1995). Many authors have taken up this subcultural theme in an effort to come to terms with the sociological significance of youth, but with mixed results. In this context, there may even be a case for arguing that, despite their economic position, young people's subcultures are less resistant to class at the beginning of the twenty-first century than ever before, and that subcultures rarely play a significant role in young people's lives.

In considering the declining influence of youth subcultures, John Epstein's (1998) contribution is of particular interest in so far as it highlights another division in the sociology of youth – that between British and American approaches to the debates in question. The historical reliance on contributions made by the Birmingham School by British sociologists has aided and abetted a strong tendency to consider British approaches to youth entirely independently from those in the United States, which in some respects have coped with the changing nature of youth more effectively. In his introduction, Epstein talks particularly about the work of Donna Gaines (1991) and Henry Giroux (1994). Gaines (1991), described by Epstein (1998) as a chronicler of a generation, investigated the everyday lives of young people in a suburban New Jersey community where four teenagers committed suicide. Gaines portrays a fatalistic generation with no future and no hope:

> In recent years many American kids have had their dreams taken from them. Their vision has been blocked, unable to move beyond next week, because the world outside is simply too much. Suicide is known as the disease of hope. Helplessness and hopelessness. Hopeless because you see no choices. Helpless because you feel that nothing you can do will ever make a difference. You feel powerless and trapped. This makes you feel worthless; you can't defend yourself.
>
> (Gaines 1991: 253–4)

Giroux is slightly more optimistic to the extent that he describes this sort of fatalism as resistance (Epstein 1998: 16), the streets providing an arena for cultural struggle, a place where young people can reject the goals of adult society. The irony here, however, as Epstein (1998) points out, is that the resistance in which young people do partake is expressed through consumerism and the mass media and as such arguably represents little more than a confirmation of the status quo. The picture drawn here is a long way from the sort of resistance associated with the melodramatic subcultures that sociologists studied in the 1960s and 1970s.

Forever young

Another controversial, and in some ways very appealing suggestion is that 'youth cultures' have lost their significance because the sorts of characteristics associated with them are now characteristic of virtually all social groups under the age of sixty. To this end Brian Appleyard (1995) suggests in the *Independent* newspaper that youth culture is now culture in its entirety. What both Appleyard (1995) and Calcutt (1998) mean by this is that popular culture, previously the preserve of young people, has now been appropriated by all age groups in order that they can 'find the iconography which describes their own lives back to them' (Calcutt 1998: 5). In this context, Calcutt goes on to argue that in a world which had its beginnings in a counter-culture which refused to accept the norms associated with adulthood, people have led their entire lives poised on the cusp of the adolescent dilemma. As such, Calcutt discusses the work of the American critic John W. Aldridge (1969) who identifies the emergence of a 'fetishization' of youth during the 1960s which developed into a lifelong excuse for immaturity and childishness, arguably personified in Britain 30 years later in the guise of Paul Gascoigne.

The childishness which is apparently amplified in Gascoigne's persona is, from this point of view, symptomatic of a broader malaise where the 'cult of youth' has apparently emerged as the avant-garde of a society which has quite simply lost the ability to move forward. Calcutt (1998) goes on to argue that people have cultivated a sense of estrangement in so far as they are alienated by the belief that they cannot actually change anything. Popular culture lives very much, therefore, for the present. Calcutt quotes Savage (1997) who argues that 'the total intensity of the moment' is 'the hallmark of youth and its culture', a suggestion which may well reinforce the suggestion that young people are essentially hedonistic (see Chapter 6). For Calcutt the abiding cultural personalities in contemporary society are the child and the victim, for they both reflect the powerless situation in which human beings find themselves in our society. This, in turn, reflects a sea change in the nature and role of youth subcultures which, I argue, should culminate in a discussion of youth *lifestyles*. The point here is that youth lifestyles, however conservative they appear to be, do not operate independently of political and social change. The benefit of this sort of approach, as I will illustrate in Chapter 2, is that it is potentially less prescriptive and less politically loaded than has previously been the case when commentators have adopted a subcultural perspective.

The implication of my criticisms of cultural approaches to the sociology of youth is that they are built on a presupposition that regards young people as essentially problematic and rebellious when that often clearly is not the case. The fact that young people are apparently equally likely to accept the status quo (and arguably always have) is just as good a reason to prioritize them as a barometer of social change (and continuity) as their predilection to oppose dominant orders. Perhaps more importantly, a grounded analysis of the apparently sober nature of youth, if we can usefully identify youth at all, represents a valuable means of coming to terms with the changing nature of the relationship between structure and agency and the way in which structures and cultures affect young people's lives in tandem. In other words, young people's experience of social life is founded on the intersection of the structural and the cultural. It is upon this intersection that *Youth Lifestyles in a Changing World* will focus.

Youth 'transitions'

Because youth lifestyles are so bound up with cultural concerns, I have so far focused on the problems inherent in over-extending conceptions of cultural aspects of young people's lives. But it is equally important to recognize that sociologists have paradoxically tended to exaggerate the impact of structural influences on young people's everyday lives and that the attraction of an in-depth understanding of youth lifestyles emanates from the way in which such a notion transcends both the cultural and the social. I will discuss the detailed restraints that commentators have identified in their discussions of youth transitions in Chapter 3, but at this stage I simply want to acknowledge that the structural arena is just as problematic as the cultural one and that the future of an effective sociology of youth very much depends on a constructive dialogue between the two.

A key term in developing any adequate understanding of young

people's lifestyles is that of 'transition', the process by which young
people somehow manage to reach 'adulthood'. This reflects the broad
concern that in recent years traditional routes into adulthood have
apparently become increasingly problematic. The concept of transition
therefore focuses on the way structures affect how young people grow
up. However, the position underlying this book as a whole is that the
over-emphasis by sociologists on what I will call the 'transition debate'
has tended to blinker them from equally important concerns about
youth lifestyles and, in particular, how such lifestyles actively engage
with the structural constraints that young people must contend with
from day to day. In some respects the tendency in recent years to adopt
a structural perspective on transitions has been counter-productive, primarily because of its failure to prioritize the actual views, experiences,
interests and perspectives of young people as they see them, in favour
of bland discussions, most commonly of trends in employment and
education patterns. The most damaging problem with the 'transition
debate' is that it has tended to take young people out of the youth equation. What I mean by this is that the sociology of youth has tended to
treat young people as troubled victims of economic and social restructuring without enough recourse to the active ways in which young
people negotiate such circumstances in the course of their everyday lives.
In this context, youth becomes little more than a term describing an
undifferentiated mass of people of similar age experiencing similar
things, when what it should be describing is a highly differentiated
group of people of similar age subject to a whole variety of experiences
depending upon a diverse range of personal circumstances.

Equally important here is an inherent problem with, or at least a contradiction of, the notion of transition, as Wyn and White (1997) point
out. While operating within a discourse that sees the transition as a fluid,
changing process, this discourse has in fact been harnessed to a static,
categorical notion of youth:

> hence, although we appear to be dealing with a concept which has
> process and change at its centre, it offers instead a perspective on
> youth as a steady progression through identifiable and predictable
> stages, to a set end point: adulthood.
>
> (Wyn and White 1997: 93)

This approach can therefore be said to over-simplify the nature of
youth experiences which are, in fact, very diverse in nature and highly
dependent upon specific personal experiences of social division and
inequality, rather than a logical stage-by-stage progression through to
the endpoint, namely, 'adulthood'. Youth is not simply another stage

in a linear life-cycle through which each and every one of us passes in the same predictable ways. Conceptions of youth transitions need to be more flexible in taking account of the multiple, spiralling nature of youth transitions which do not represent a fixed point at all, but rather a plethora of *transitional transitions*. Youth is related to age, but is not determined by it. Sociologists of youth therefore need to focus not on the characteristics of young people of a particular age group, but rather on the construction of youth as a way of life or a lifestyle constructed through social processes such as family relationships, the labour market, schooling and training, but often expressed through cultural means. I am advocating a socio-cultural interpretation of youth that sees the process of youth as being dependent on the active endowment of meaning within it by young people. Power structures and relationships do exist, but what is exciting about those relationships for the sociologist is the way in which young people negotiate with and interpret those structures and relationships.

The suggestion here is not that traditional notions of the transition are entirely redundant, but that those notions need to be deployed far more imaginatively and pro-actively. The static conception of transitions currently adopted by most youth studies' commentators is only useful in so far as it provides a way of conceptualizing the 'big picture' (Wyn and Whyte 1997). But the concept falls down when applied too closely to the actualities and complexities of young people's everyday lives, which it simply cannot cater for adequately. Indeed, it is almost as if sociologists of youth are actively afraid of the challenging prospect of coming to terms with the depth and richness of youth experience. Perhaps they fear that the limitations of the conceptual tools on which they have depended for decades might be exposed, and the very authenticity of the sociology of youth may itself be threatened. The problem then, as Furlong and Cartmel (1997) note, is that young people's biographies are simply too diverse for the debate over youth transitions to continue as it has done over the past twenty or so years. Perhaps more significant, however, is Williamson's (1997a: 16) observation that 'rather too much youth research has served the theoretical positions of its writers than the articulated needs of the young people who have been the subject of that research'.

Navigating a way forward

The division between cultural and structural conceptions of youth is maintained by a tendency to over-theorize the former approach and over-research the latter. Of particular concern here is the fact that these two types of approach have remained almost entirely independent when young people's actual experience of cultural and social spheres is almost entirely *inter*dependent. The consequence of all this is that the sociology of youth has a very partial handle on what it is to be a young person at the end of the twentieth century. In other words, the everyday experience of young people in contemporary society centres on the point of contact between these two spheres, and yet sociologists, often for instrumental reasons, continue to insist on studying them as separate entities.

Amid such confusion, some commentators have argued that the very notion of youth is redundant in the sense that young people are seen to be reacting to a variety of social forces which are not necessarily peculiar to people in their particular age group; they argue that sociologists should make those social forces rather than young people themselves their starting point (see Jeffs and Smith 1998). I would suggest that this sort of approach underestimates the commonalities which young people experience in their everyday lives and that a first stage in dealing with this problem should be to identify appropriate conceptual tools that can transcend the divide identified above. The intention of *Youth Lifestyles in a Changing World* is therefore to highlight the potential for advancing the sociology of youth by focusing on youth lifestyles as an active arena within which the everyday struggles associated with the dialectical relationship between structure and agency can be worked out.

Structure of the book

To the above end, in Chapter 2 I outline sociological conceptions of 'lifestyle' before reflecting on how that particular notion might help to enliven our understanding of young people's relationship with social change in the context of debates surrounding the relationship between structure and agency. I therefore suggest that an understanding of consumer lifestyles is particularly salient to what young people's lives are all about as we move into the twenty-first century.

In Chapter 3 I reiterate my argument that young people's lifestyles cannot be adequately understood without reference to the structural contexts in which they operate. Here, I focus in particular on education and employment as the two most important arenas in which young people struggle to establish themselves as citizens in a world in which they continue to be marginalized. However, I go on to argue that structural influences on young people's lives can only be fully comprehended if the cultural contexts in which they are contextualized are actively addressed.

My suggestion in Chapter 4 is therefore that the apparent marginalization of young people cannot be understood without a thorough understanding of social change and the cultural contexts in which young people interpret such change. In this context I prioritize discussions of post-modern fragmentation, risk society and globalization. All three of these areas affect young people's experience of social change through processes of individualization which have, in turn, served to undermine the traditional nature of the youth experience, while threatening the orthodoxy of the ways in which sociologists have tended to address these questions in the past.

The next two chapters are, in effect, case studies in which I examine particular aspects of young people's lives that many commentators have identified as being fundamental to their relationship with a changing world. In Chapter 5 I consider the nature of young people's relationship with and consumption of the mass media. Are they controlled by it, or do they actively mould it to their own ends? I go on to identify young people's use of the electronic media as being an especially important aspect of their lifestyles, particularly in relation to representations of consumer culture. Chapter 6 discusses in detail what is arguably one of the most important expressions of the changing nature of youth culture, namely rave. In particular, this chapter considers how far rave simply represents the acceptance on the part of young people of dominant ideological codes, and most especially that of consumerism as a way of life. Is rave anything more than a celebration of hedonism, a temporary window of escape from a culture that young people are actively propping up?

Taking this discussion of hedonism one step further, Chapter 7 focuses on the emergence of young people as consumers, arguing that consumption is the primary arena within which young people relate to and reproduce social change. Can youth consumption be 'authentic' and what role does consumption have in constructing young people's identities? This is a question I address empirically in Chapter 8 which looks at the construction of young people's lifestyles in context through a series of group interviews with young people. This provides a useful means of actively coming to terms with what constitutes youth lifestyles in a changing world.

Chapter 9 draws the above threads together in arguing that young people's lifestyles do indeed represent an invaluable means of coming to terms with their own changing relationship with social, cultural and structural change. In this context the construction of young people's identities is highlighted as a particularly important issue and one that sociologists of youth may need to prioritize if they are to bring their area of study kicking, screaming and raving into the twenty-first century.

This book aims to present a new perspective on young people's relationship to social change. It represents an attempt to avoid a tendency elsewhere in the literature to get bogged down in rather dry and often unrevealing discussions of youth inequality and disadvantage, while being equally concerned to give a more grounded basis to some of the more obtuse and often remote approaches to cultural aspects of young people's lives. Young people are indeed barometers of social change, but they do not simply reflect such change; they actively and consciously partake in it. If *Youth Lifestyles in a Changing World* can provide more than merely a flavour of what it means to be a young person at the beginning of the new millennium, while questioning the role that sociology should play in monitoring such meanings, then it will have gone some way towards achieving its aim.

Recommended reading

Epstein, Jonathon, S. (ed.) (1998) *Youth Culture: Identity in a Postmodern World*. Oxford: Blackwell.
   A collection of American articles about young people's experience of a postmodern world. Provides a useful insight into the changing nature of 'youth culture'.
Thornton, Sarah (1997) *Club Cultures: Music, Media and Subcultural Capital*. Cambridge: Polity.
   An insightful and theoretically sound analysis of young people's consumption of club cultures, and an example of a more cultural approach to the youth question.
Widdicombe, S. and Wooffitt, R. (1995) *The Language of Youth Subcultures*. London: Harvester Wheatsheaf.
   Provides a useful critique of traditional approaches to subcultures that have tended to neglect mainstream youth in favour of a sociology of the melodramatic.
Wyn, Johanna and White, Rob (1997) *Rethinking Youth*. London: Sage.
   This Australian text provides one of the most insightful discussions of what it currently means to be a young person and how sociologists need to adapt in this context.

2
LIVING LIFESTYLES

It is tempting to assume that the nature of youth or young people's lifestyles has radically altered in recent years. This comes, at least partly, from sentimental memories of a lost youth most commonly expressed as 'it wasn't like this in my day'. If you add this general (and often unsubstantiated) feeling to a concomitant one that the world in general is changing at a breathtaking pace, you have a ready-made recipe for a predetermined conception of what it is to be a young person at the beginning of the twenty-first century. This book will propose that the world has indeed changed radically in recent decades and that lifestyles and, in particular, consumer lifestyles have played an increasingly important role in cementing such change, but also that however sentimental one might get about one's own youth, young people's lifestyles are essentially more paradoxical in terms of the juxtaposition of the predictable and the unpredictable than they ever have been in the past. In this chapter I will concentrate on outlining the value of a discussion of 'lifestyles', notably in the context of the structure and agency debate where the work of Anthony Giddens and Pierre Bourdieu is especially instructive. I will then discuss the value of addressing lifestyles as lived, identity-forming and most often consumer-based entities, before concluding with a more detailed discussion of what constitutes young people's lifestyles.

In the above context, it could be argued that the declining value of the notion of subculture as discussed in Chapter 1, and as outlined by

Muggleton (1997), demands the use of an alternative conceptual focus, and that that focus should be youth *lifestyles*. Muggleton points out that youth lifestyles appear currently to be more individualistic than they are subcultural: 'For post-subculturalists, the trappings of spectacular style are their right of admission to a costume party, a masquerade, a hedonistic escape into a Blitz Culture fantasy characterized by political indifference' (p. 200). In this respect then, it is the masquerade of youth with which this book is concerned and such a masquerade is perhaps best researched through a concerted understanding of what constitutes young people's lifestyles. In effect, as Chaney (1996: 11) points out, lifestyles can be described as 'functional responses to modernity'. Lifestyles, then, are an active expression of not only the relationship between the individual and society and structure and agency, but also people's relationship to social change.

Defining 'lifestyle'

In a world where individual lifestyles appear to have more prescience in young people's lives than specific subcultural agendas, it is necessary to define exactly what is meant by the term 'lifestyle' and to identify more precisely what sociological value it has as a conceptual tool. It is worth noting for instance, that a lot of the social scientific work on lifestyles has tended to be associated with health and the degree to which people, and often young people, are 'healthy' (e.g. Prokhorov *et al.* 1993). This book incorporates a broader definition of lifestyles which is more concerned with young people's active expression of a 'way of life'.

To illustrate the difficulties in accurately defining what it is that constitutes a 'lifestyle' it is useful to turn to Michael Sobel (1981) and the influences on his work – his being one of the most important contributions to the debate on the relationship between lifestyles and social structure. Sobel's core argument is that too often the term 'lifestyle' has been used in a lackadaisical fashion and that it needs to be constructed on more focused and sociologically situated foundations if it is to have any true meaning. So what does Sobel mean when he talks about 'lifestyles'? Interestingly, he notes that the 'founding fathers' of sociology, Marx and Weber, used the term 'lifestyle' as a *derived* rather than a primary concept. Certainly, Marx and Weber's concern for questions of lifestyle tend to be implicit and are not developed in any thoroughgoing fashion. Marx would describe lifestyle as the individual's objective position in the production process: the structure that loosely shapes values and attitudes and determines critical life experiences. This is an important point to make in the context of this book for its underlying argument is that the structures that shape young people's values and attitudes have manifestly changed in recent decades. As such, youth lifestyles amount to increasingly significant sociological indicators in their own right. Equally significant, as Sobel notes, is Weber's recognition that

> The decisive role of a 'style of life' in status 'honor' means that status groups are the specific bearers of all 'conventions'. In whatever way it be manifest, all 'stylization' of life either originates in status groups or is at least conserved by them.
>
> (Weber 1966: 26)

Weber's emphasis here tends to be on the way in which class stratifies status groups according to the principles of their consumption of goods as represented by special 'styles of life' (Weber 1966: 27). Status plays a key role in stratifying society and is in turn expressed through different groups' lifestyles. But the important point, as Sobel (1981) points out, is that Weber's treatment of lifestyle as we perceive it today is very much *derivative* of class. In Weber's analysis lifestyle does not play a key role in the construction of social life in its own right.

The argument here is that although class continues to play an important role in the construction of identities, that role is not so all-powerful as to *determine* young people's lifestyles, as authors such as Furlong and Cartmel (1997) appear to imply. The construction of lifestyles is an interactive process which includes areas of social life, such as fun and pleasure, to which sociologists have traditionally paid scant attention (Moorhouse 1989). Moorhouse takes up this debate in his critique of approaches to the work-leisure dynamic. He argues that questions of status and lifestyle potentially represent a means of bridging employment and non-employment and hence of coming to terms with the complexities of social life at the beginning of the twenty-first century.

As Reimer (1995) argues, various other 'classic' authors, including Veblen and Simmel, have picked up on certain aspects of lifestyles but without always referring to the term directly. Indeed, during the first half of the twentieth century the concept of lifestyle was neglected, partly perhaps because of the commercial connotation implied (see Reimer 1995: 122). It was not until the 1980s that the concept regained any sort of popularity, and Reimer argues that it has since enjoyed something of a renaissance. Four main reasons can be identified for this, the first two being based on changes in the social structure which, in turn, have resulted in changes in people's ways of life, and the other two reasons being more to do with how academics have set about dealing with such changes:

1 Processes of individualization resulting, especially among young people, in greater degrees of freedom and choice in a rapidly changing world.
2 The growth of a new middle class who are well educated and well represented in service or communications professions. This group is apparently entertainment and consumption-oriented and would include 'young urban professionals' or 'yuppies'.
3 The increasingly high academic profile of debates concerning post-modernity in which the emergence of new values and lifestyles appear to play a key role.
4 The influential contribution of Pierre Bourdieu's work on lifestyles and, in particular, his book *Distinction* (see Reimer 1995).

Regardless of the above changes in the structure of social life and the academic conception of these changes, the key concern, as Reimer goes on to point out, is

> how people act and create meaning in everyday life, especially in those areas where one can act more independently. Lifestyle is . . . the specific pattern of everyday activities that characterizes an individual. Each individual's lifestyle is unique: it is not identical to anyone else's. But at the same time, lifestyles orient themselves towards the common and the social . . . We choose lifestyles in relation to other people . . . Analyses of lifestyles should therefore often address similarities and differences between groups of individuals rather than towards similarities and differences between groups.
> (Reimer 1995: 124–5)

Part of the appeal of the notion of lifestyle therefore lies in the way in which it actively addresses the duality of structure and agency.

Structure and agency

Before I discuss ways in which the notion of lifestyle appears to bridge debates over structure and agency, I want to highlight why such a debate is so important to sociologists. The relationship between structure and agency is a pivotal concern of contemporary social theory, and arguably has always been *the* key sociological concern (Archer 1995). By confronting the structure and agency problem, Archer (1995: 65) argues that sociologists are in fact addressing 'the most pressing social problem of the human condition'. This point is acutely evident at an everyday experiential level, where we see that life is actively constituted by the contrary feeling that the individual is both free and yet somehow simultaneously constrained. It is arguably this feeling that lies at the heart of young people's experience of social life.

Discussing in particular the influence of the 'macro-micro' issue on contemporary sociological thought, Layder (1994) points out that the structure and agency dualism, and the debate that surrounds it, highlight the fact that people are 'agents' in the social world; they are actively able to do things which affect the everyday social relationships in which they are embedded. As far as this book is concerned, the value of the structure/agency debate is to highlight the role of everyday social interactions and encounters in the construction of social worlds, while simultaneously acknowledging the way in which wider social contexts influence such interactions. Society, then, is inseparable from its human components because the very existence of that society depends upon human activities. What society is, at any given time, depends upon those activities. On the other hand, individuals are not immutable as social agents, because existence as social beings is also affected by the experience of the society in which people live, and by their efforts to transform that society (Archer 1995). The suggestion here is that there is a possibility that the arena within which young people adapt to/transform that society is the arena of 'lifestyles'. Before I consider this point I want to discuss two particularly useful approaches to the question of structure and agency in more depth.

Anthony Giddens' theory of structuration

The author who is perhaps most synonymous with discussions of structure and agency is Anthony Giddens. Giddens' theory of structuration amounts to one of the most accomplished, if empirically under-utilized, approaches to the structure and agency debate (see Bryant and Jary 1991). Giddens (1976), as Blaikie (1993) notes, sees the production and reproduction of society as an accomplishment of social actors. His notion of the duality of structure, the idea that social structures are both the conditions and the consequences of social interaction, is central to his structuration theory. As such, 'social structures are both constituted *by* human agency, and yet at the same time are the very *medium* of this constitution' (Giddens 1976: 121) [emphasis in the original].

In this sense, all social action involves structure and all structure involves human action. The human actor is therefore reflexive and monitors the flow of activities in which he or she is involved, alongside basic structural conditions. Whereas Giddens would argue that sociology has traditionally exaggerated the constraining nature of structures, he in fact sees structure as both constraining *and* enabling. Human beings are creative and responsive agents involved in a continual flow of conduct (see Ritzer 1992). In this sense, Giddens sees structures as rules and resources that actors draw upon as they produce and reproduce society in their everyday actions. By reflecting on their own behaviour, people are always capable, to some extent, of influencing and transforming their social situations.

What Giddens' structuration theory attempts to do, then, is to combine an understanding of strategic conduct with that of institutional analysis (i.e. the recurring patterns of interaction in a social system that embody the social structure). Giddens (1984) identifies three structural dimensions of social systems: signification, domination and legitimation. He suggests that signification is fundamentally structured through language, in the sense that human beings negotiate meaning through communication and interaction. In this respect, Giddens agrees with the symbolic interactionists. As individuals, people bring 'interpretive schemes' to bear on social events and make sense of the social world by applying meanings. However, such meaning is also institutionalized in as much as people draw on socially available meanings to make sense of what they do. In turn, Giddens' notion of domination draws upon ideas about power, which he sees not so much as being an impersonal characteristic of social structures, but more as a social resource: 'By authorisation I refer to capabilities which generate command over persons and by "allocation" I refer to capabilities which generate command over objects or other material phenomena' (Giddens 1984: 32). Material objects are therefore transformed into resources and, in effect, become codes and normative sanctions. The third aspect of Giddens' classification is legitimation: the contention that every society has a set of institutionalized norms and values that uphold particular ways of doing things by making them appear to be legitimate. However, Giddens argues that this does not necessarily lead to the assumption that the norms which legitimate social structures are widely accepted.

Bearing the above three notions in mind, Giddens argues that people engage in strategic conduct while drawing upon interpretative schemes, facilities and resources, and norms and values. It is through such action that society functions and, whether intentionally or unintentionally, social structure is reproduced. What Giddens is arguing, then, is that

> there is no such thing as a distinctive type of 'structural explanation' in the social sciences. All explanations will involve at least

implicit reference to both the purposive, reasoning behaviour of agents and to its intersection with the constraining and enabling features of the social and material contexts of that behaviour.

(Giddens 1984: 178–9)

In this context, identity is very much a negotiation between the individual and the social group. As such, Giddens' analysis has some important implications for any discussion of the role of lifestyle in constructing young people's lives.

Giddens discusses the experience of self-identity in the context of the massive 'intensional and extensional changes' which are set into being by the onset of modernity. However, he also argues that it is misleading to suggest that contextual diversity in everyday life will necessarily promote a fragmented self. An integrated self is equally seen as a possibility, depending upon the ways in which individuals use the cultural resources at their disposal. The suggestion here is that an individual uses such resources through the everyday interpretation and negotiation of lifestyles. For Giddens, the narrative of the self is the product of a balance between structural influences on everyday life, such as standardized consumption patterns, and the personal appropriation of such influences.

Pierre Bourdieu's theory of structuration

Pierre Bourdieu presents a theory of consumption and consumer lifestyles premised on the structure and agency debate. Like Giddens, Bourdieu (1984) criticizes the extremities of structural and interactionist approaches to social life, arguing that they are essentially reductionist in their respective outlooks. Pivotal to this theory is Bourdieu's notion of the 'habitus', the everyday knowledge or cultural capital, that reflects the routine experience of appropriate behaviour in particular cultures and subcultures. Bourdieu sees human experience as being determined by the habitus. What is interesting about Bourdieu's work, notably in *Distinction*, an empirical study of consumption in France in the 1960s and 1970s, is his insistence that consumers are not merely products of social structures. However, as Lee (1993) points out, Bourdieu does not adopt the opposite position by arguing that social action is entirely voluntary. Rather, by using the concept of the 'habitus', Bourdieu succeeds, at least partially, in presenting a balanced conception of the individual. He transcends the ideology of both individualism and subjectivism, as Branson and Miller (1991) note, by seeing individuals as the clue, as objects of empirical study, to an understanding which lies *beyond* the individual. Bourdieu defines the habitus as providing a group-distinctive framework of social cognition and interpretation – the mental structures which individuals carry around in their heads, in order that they can deal with the world.

> Life-styles are thus the systematic products of habitus, which, perceived in their mutual relations through the schemes of the habitus, become sign systems that are socially qualified (as 'distinguished', 'vulgar' etc.) The dialectic of conditions and habitus is the basis of an alchemy which transforms the distribution of capital, the balance-sheet of a power relation, into a system of perceived differences, distinctive properties, that is, a distribution of symbolic capital, legitimate capital, whose objective truth is misrecognized.
>
> (Bourdieu 1984: 172)

Bourdieu (1984) suggests that the habitus is in fact instigated from early childhood through interaction with family and various other social agents and, as Lee (1993) points out, it is the embodiment of the cultural dispositions and sensibilities which structure group behaviour. This simultaneously allows group members a mechanism for structuring their own personal social experience. As such, Craik (1994) sees particular resonance for the term in the context of fashion, the clothing of the body being a particularly important and active means of constructing and presenting a bodily self.

Bourdieu's vision of culture is a theory of social practices (see Waters 1994). Culture is separate from people as individuals and, as such, constrains people, and yet at the same time is constructed through human agency. Here, Bourdieu (1984) is keen to assert that the position a person has in a structure does not in itself generate a way of life. Members of a social group may act, but they do so as agents of social action not as mirrors of the group to which they belong. An individual's symbolic activity, often expressed through modes of consumption is therefore relatively autonomous (see Bocock 1993). Consumption therefore serves as a means of establishing, as opposed to merely expressing, variations between social groups. Human beings are motivated by the need to reproduce a collective pattern of preferences based on class demarcation. Cultural capital is crucial in this respect: different classes are qualified, educationally, to take advantage of different aspects of symbolic capital. The dominant classes therefore demonstrate their superiority through access to high culture. The habitus is reproduced between generations, and thereby generates the schemes by which cultural objects are classified and differentiated (Waters 1994). Class differences are inscribed in individuals as distinctions in taste. In effect, an individual's social experience is structured by what the social group sees as being the legitimate way to behave and consume, according to the correct classifications of taste.

Reimer suggests that Bourdieu's major contribution to sociological debates lies in an understanding of what lies behind the organization of everyday life, namely the processes involved in having culturally appropriate forms of taste. From this point of view, lifestyles are about behaving in culturally accepted ways, depending upon the cultural capital of the person concerned: the more cultural capital you have, the more extravagant your lifestyle is likely to be. The crucial point, however, is that there is a hierarchy of taste whereby certain activities are deemed more culturally appropriate than others. Lifestyles therefore play an active role in upholding social hierarchies because some people have more access to cultural (and economic) capital than others. In effect then, group contexts and influences play a key role in the construction of people's lifestyles:

> In identifying what is worthy of being seen and the right way to see it, they are aided by their whole social group . . . and by the whole corporation of critics mandated by the group to produce legitimate classifications and the discourse necessarily accompanying any artistic enjoyment worthy of the name.
>
> (Bourdieu 1984: 28)

As Reimer (1995) suggests, Bourdieu's work has been criticized on two main fronts: first, that his research was culturally bound up with the specific lifestyles associated with France in the 1960s, and second, that his theory is overly deterministic because of his argument that cultural products direct how people respond to one another. However, Bourdieu, like Giddens, has provided sociology, and more specifically the sociology of youth, with some useful tools that may well provide a means of deciphering the relationship between structure and agency. Both authors' conception of lifestyles may well prove to be especially useful in this regard.

Lifestyle and identity

Putting to one side any criticisms of Bourdieu's contribution to the debate over the sociological significance of the notion of 'lifestyle', it is now necessary to come to some preliminary conclusions about what lifestyle means in the context of the above debates concerning structure and agency. The following quotations sum up quite nicely what constitutes the sociological significance of 'lifestyles' and the associated conceptions of structure, agency and identity:

> A lifestyle enclave is formed by people who share some feature of private life. Members of a lifestyle enclave express their identity through shared patterns of appearance, consumption, and leisure activities, which often serve to differentiate them sharply from those with other lifestyles.
>
> (Bellah *et al.* 1985: 355)

> A lifestyle is a distinctive set of shared patterns of tangible behaviour that is organized around a set of coherent interests or social conditions or both, that is explained and justified by a set of related values, attitudes, and orientation and that, under certain conditions, becomes the basis for a separate, common social identity for its participants.
>
> (Stebbins 1997: 350)

A couple of key points emerge from the above quotations: first, the centrality of the notion of identity, and second, how identities are constructed in social contexts. The above quotations are entirely pertinent to the argument running through this book, namely that not only have the conditions underlying young people's values and attitudes changed but the actual materialization of such a change is evident primarily through a delicate balancing act between the construction of individuality and relationships constructed in groups. In other words, lifestyles are not entirely individual in nature but are constructed through affiliation and negotiation, by the active integration of the individual and society, which are constantly, as Giddens would argue, reproduced through each other.

Of more immediate interest here, however, is the relationship between lifestyles and identity which has perhaps been most effectively discussed by the Swedish researchers Thomas Johansson and Frederik Miegel (1992). Johansson and Miegel recognize that the constant change in societal and cultural values held by particular social groups has a key role to play in influencing individual identities. Although recognizing that class is an important factor in the formation of lifestyles, Johansson and Miegel maintain that the core of a lifestyle is to be found in the identity of the individual. Dividing the concept of identity into three different but interrelated types – personal, social and cultural – the authors argue that the last is the most significant for the construction of a person's lifestyle. Adapting Bourdieu's (1984) notion of habitus, Johansson and Miegel (1992) stress the importance of internalizing abstract culture and of mediating between societal structures and subjective interpretations of and attitudes towards these situations. Most importantly, lifestyles have in this context become arguably less and less determined by structural and positional conditions and more and more determined by how an individual's identity relates to those conditions. Thus, it is through an individual's habitus that he or she constructs an awareness of his or her own position within different societal and cultural systems (see Bourdieu 1984). According to Johansson and Miegel, it is through cultural identity that an individual develops individual values, style, cultural taste and hence lifestyle. It does not follow, however, that personal and social identity are irrelevant in this respect. Indeed, the two authors argue that identity cannot be taken to be equivalent to cultural consumption, but that cultural consumption, however significant, is influenced by social position and the individual's unique personal identity.

The problem with analyses of lifestyles and also of identity, as Johansson and Miegel (1992) point out, has been that commentators have tended to make assumptions about people's identities based on one component of that identity. In other words, there has been a temptation to generalize about a person's identity in its entirety when, for instance, it may only be their cultural identity that is being altered at any point in time. If a young person takes on aspects of a rave-inspired cultural identity, for example, it does not necessarily follow that his or her personal or social identity will be affected as much as his or her cultural one. It is therefore important to note that the most unstable component of identity is cultural and thus dramatic changes in lifestyles may all too easily be exaggerated. The real point here is that any discussion of contemporary lifestyles is closely bound up with one of the most important themes in classical and modern sociology, the complex relationship between the individual and society. From this point of view, lifestyles are no longer exclusively determined by social status as related to notions of class, gender, ethnicity and sexuality, for example, and yet

> Neither are lifestyles equivalent to total freedom for individuals in the choice of values, attitudes and actions, even though this freedom may be increased. The core of lifestyle, therefore, is located in cultural identity. Whereas the personal identity is non-individual, cultural identity can be both individual or non-individual . . . in order to comprehend lifestyle in contemporary Western societies,

one must understand the dynamic relation between the individual and society.

(Johansson and Miegel 1992: 78–9)

There may well be a valid argument for suggesting that the notion of lifestyle should be closely bound up with the question of identity (see Chapter 9). As individuals, people appear to be concerned with establishing a sense of who they are, both individually and as part of the wider world (Plummer 1981). In this context, a lifestyle can be described as the outward expression of an identity. If we are to accept the contention that youth represents a key period in the construction of people's identities, then lifestyles should become a key focus for sociological investigation in the sense that lifestyles actively express young people's relationships with their social world. Although Plummer talks specifically about the process of incorporating gayness into an overall lifestyle pattern, his arguments are equally pertinent to a more general sociology of lifestyles. Lifestyles are the outward social expression of specific identity positions. At this point, it is worth referring back to Weber who 'equates leisure practice with a subjectively meaningful affiliation to a specific value position, and . . . defines the lifestyle attached to a given form as a symbolic expression of power' (Rojek 1985: 73). In other words, people actively differentiate themselves from others through 'honorific' preferences (Rojek 1985: 74).

Lifestyles as *lived* cultures

Another crucial theme to pick up on at this stage is the fact that lifestyles are formed in contrast to, or at least in respect of a relationship with, a dominant culture. Lifestyles are, in effect, lived cultures in which individuals actively express their identities but do so in direct relation to their position as regards the dominant culture. In Sobel's (1983) words, a lifestyle can be conceptualized as 'a set of observable behavioral choices that individuals make' (p. 521). Most importantly, the construction of lifestyle is an active social and control process to the extent that 'each individual may be viewed as a producer of his or her lifestyle, and it is through this creative participation in the normative order that individuals may generate status, meaning and self-esteem' (p. 521).

Of particular importance here, however, is Sobel's (1983) contention that as a sociological notion 'lifestyle' may surpass other bases of deference. For instance, the influence of work in constructing who a person is, is arguably less important and more instrumental than it was in the past. But this is even more the case for young people who often do not have a stable work environment upon which they can construct positive conceptions of themselves (see Chapter 3). In this context, lifestyle is likely to play more of a central role in how people perceive themselves, precisely because the cultural arena within which lifestyles are largely constructed play a more immediate role in their lives.

Many of the authors I have discussed during the course of this chapter have illustrated that the notion of lifestyle is a highly contested one. A central problem is that the notion of lifestyle tends to be defined simply as a mode of living, thereby encouraging a very ad hoc and unspecific discussion of the term. Indeed, 'the application of the label is not just confusing and inappropriate; it also distorts, by means of gross over-simplification, the nature of descriptive reality' (Sobel 1981: 29). The key point here is that if the notion of lifestyle is to have any sort of sociological value it needs to be addressed in specific contexts through the analysis of the specific meanings constructed by agents of social life and how they relate to the dominant culture. In other words, an adequate conceptualization lies in a grounded analysis of how people conduct their lives and what they perceive their lifestyles to be. In terms of the subject matter of this book, assumptions cannot be made about what it is that constitutes youth lifestyles; youth lifestyles can only be analysed through the meanings which people invest in those lifestyles. Those lifestyles should be physically observable and 'deducible from observation over which an individual has considerable discretionary power' (Sobel 1981: 166). Sobel's position on this point is summed up nicely in the following quotation:

> lifestyle is important because it manifests both social and individual identity, because lifestyle has become an increasingly important center of meaning, in short, because the creation of lifestyle itself is a time-intensive activity with a heavy investment of ego. In this context, the modern significance of a lifestyle may arise as a solution to the existential problems of boredom, meaninglessness, and lack of control, problems created by the confluence of affluence and the destruction of the traditional centers of meaning, religion, work, family, and the community.
>
> (Sobel 1991: 171)

Sobel's position might well be over-romanticized in the sense that he does tend to imply a yearning for a forgotten past, but it is also significant because it expresses the fact that lifestyles are historical constructs that change over time. Lifestyles actively express the tensions that exist between structure and agency and how that relationship changes over time. In this context, Giddens' (1991) definition is particularly useful: 'A lifestyle can be defined as a more or less integrated set of practices which an individual embraces, not only because such practices fulfil utilitarian needs, but because they give material form to a particular form of self-identity' (p. 81).

Consumer lifestyles

Lifestyles can effectively be described as the material expression of an individual's identity. An underlying concern of this book is that the material form of self-identity to which Giddens refers is quite often constituted through consumer goods and, although not representing the source of that identity, such goods might well represent the vehicle upon which that identity is constructed. Of most importance is the recognition that young people are potentially more willing and active subjects in the creation of their own lifestyles than they may have been in the past, and consumption may well provide a useful resource in this context. Chaney (1996) argues that while consumerism played a key role in the social development of modernity, it was only towards the end of the nineteenth century and at the beginning of the twentieth century that a consumer culture with its emphasis on the pursuit of style began to emerge in its own right. It was in this historical context that consumption emerged as a key component of late twentieth-century lifestyles. But perhaps more interesting as far as youth lifestyles are concerned, Chaney quotes material collected for the Mintel (1988) report on British lifestyles in which evidence seems to suggest that the period between childhood and the assumption of full adult responsibility appears to be being extended. This reflects the increasingly uncertain nature of the employment market and the related expansion in education, but also as Chaney (1996) points out, the determination of young people to be 'free' as long as possible. Arguably, people's roles as consumers are becoming increasingly important as a reflection of broader social change within which consumerism has come to enjoy a higher social profile. This is likely to be especially true of young people who are often at the cutting edge of cultural change. This is one of the reasons why Chaney (1996) advocates a re-evaluation of material culture 'away from the immediate monetary value of objects and towards their social or cultural value . . . the currency of lifestyles is the symbolic meaning of artefacts, that is, what they are seen to represent over and above their manifest identity' (p. 43).

The freedom to be 'free' plays a key part in the construction of young people's social lives and in the construction of their identities. Indeed, as Miller (1987) points out, consumer artefacts are not inherently meaningful: they derive their meaning from the ways in which people use them in an active process of self-creation. The following quotation from Chaney (1996: 156–7) sums up nicely the relationship between lifestyles and consumption:

> lifestyles have been . . . ways of enacting new forms of identity. The creative energies involved in articulating and sustaining new patterns of social association are in a very profound sense a form of design, a way of working and using the symbolic profusion of material culture in mass society to constitute new cultural forms.

In effect then, lifestyles are constructed *through* consumption which is in itself the primary indicator of lifestyles in a changing world. Consumption, as Sobel (1981: 47) notes, is 'the activity that best captures what is meant by lifestyle'.

One author who has taken up this theme in the context of debates concerning post-modernity is Mike Featherstone (1987, 1991). Featherstone argues that the more restricted sociological definition of lifestyle as outlined by authors such as Sobel has given way to a more individualistic style-conscious and therefore apparently less sociological type of lifestyle reflective of life in a consumer culture. Featherstone quotes Ewen and Ewen's (1982: 249–51) much touted phrases, 'Today there is no fashion: there are only fashions . . . No rules, only choices . . . Everyone can be anyone.' Featherstone's (1991) argument is basically that lifestyles are less fixed than they have been in the past and he therefore asks:

> What does it mean to suggest that long-held fashion codes have been violated, that there is a war against uniformity, a surfeit of difference which results in a loss of meaning? The implication is that we are moving towards a society without fixed status groups in which the adoption of styles of life (manifest in choice of clothes, leisure activities, consumer goods, bodily dispositions) which are fixed to specific groups have been surpassed. This apparent movement towards a post-modern consumer culture based upon a profusion of information and proliferation of images which cannot be ultimately stabilized, or hierarchized into a system which correlates to fixed social divisions, would further suggest the irrelevance of social divisions and ultimately the end of the social as a significant reference point.
>
> (p. 83)

It is perhaps for this reason that lifestyle has remained an under-utilized notion. There is an in-built assumption in the literature that lifestyles are inherently flexible and undergoing a process of constant change, and therefore somehow beyond the remit of the sociological enterprise. In fact, this is manifestly not the case, as the discussion of youth lifestyles throughout this book will illustrate. But in the meantime I need to clarify further the relationship between lifestyles and consumption. It would be misleading to suggest that lifestyles are merely a mirror-image of consumption habits. However, it *would* be reasonable to suggest that consumption provides a language or code within which lifestyles are constructed. Status, consumption and lifestyles are, in this respect, intimately related. As I will show in Chapter 7, consumption provides the basis upon which lifestyles express membership of a social group. The important point here is that the nature of lifestyles have changed to the extent that the notion itself is of more sociological significance than it ever has been before. More pertinently, lifestyles have become an especially significant indicator of changes in young people's lives. Although the word 'lifestyle' is commonly used as a marketing-generated attribution of social class, and as a reaction to the apparent breakdown of traditional social classes, these sorts of approaches are rather simplistic in tending to focus merely on how individuals allocate income (see Solomon *et al.* 1999). The suggestion here is that if a more sophisticated notion of lifestyle is developed, it will help us to understand the complex nature of social life in a constantly changing world and, in particular, how young people relate to such change.

Young people's lifestyles

The nature of young people's lifestyles has generally been addressed by sociologists of youth in an indirect fashion (with reference to subcultures and youth cultures rather than lifestyles *per se*) and few commentators have considered the factors influencing young people's lifestyles and thus their psycho-social significance. Perhaps the most significant author in this respect is Paul Willis (1990) and his discussion of symbolic capital and common culture. Willis argues that we are all cultural producers in some shape or form and that young people respond in all sorts of positive and creative ways to the various symbolic stimuli that surround them. Significantly, 'cultural commodities enhance and greatly increase the informal possibilities of cultural creativity and are now inextricably tangled up with them' (p. 131).

Such developments reflect a broader process whereby work arguably has less and less intrinsic value beyond that as a means for livelihood and leisure. As part of a historical undermining of legitimate sources of social meaning and membership, there no longer apparently exists any real sense of a truly shared or 'whole' culture, for the whole process of identity construction is potentially more complex. From this point of view, young people construct their lifestyles in a very creative fashion which allows them to discover new possibilities for the creative continuum that exists between notions of what is 'passive' and what is 'active'. As far as the construction of consumer lifestyles is concerned, Willis argues that young people are quite capable of transforming the politics of consumption for their own ends and, in turn, quite capable of assessing critically what consumer culture has to offer them. In short, Willis sees culture as lived practice. He sees an individual's identity as flowing from symbolic exchange through which social actors emerge. Young people do not buy consumer goods passively or uncritically but transform, appropriate and recontextualize meanings. Willis (1990: 27) vehemently advocates a move towards an interpretation of 'the movement of the real world'. It can be argued then that young people's lifestyles represent the arena within which such movement is undertaken.

One author who does consider the issue of youth lifestyles somewhat more directly is Christine Griffin (1993). Griffin notes that the mainstream literature tends to see young people's consumption in terms of 'lifestyles', 'choice' and 'freedom' to the extent that 'part of the process of transition to adulthood for "normal" young people involves learning to make "appropriate lifestyle choices", whilst needing "protection" from the rigours of unfettered consumer capitalism' (Griffin 1993: 139). As noted in Chapter 1, there are significant problems involved in using notions of 'youth culture' and 'subculture' in discussions of young people, particularly in terms of the assumptions that such notions hold about young people's lives. Jenkins (1983) therefore prefers to prioritize the notion of 'lifestyle' and justifies this position by pointing out that the study of lifestyle 'directs attention away from the cultural realm of meaning and towards the emphasis on practice' (p. 41). What Jenkins means by this is that there is a tendency to comprehend cultural expressions of social life independently of their wider social context:

> Such an account must take as problematic that mixture of individual practice and institutional, or other, constraint which constitutes the process of the production and reproduction of social reality. In addition, however, such an account of cultural

reproduction must allow for the description and analysis of the institutions and patterns of events which may be loosely thought of as a social structure – and which are reproduced in practice – without reifying that concept or equipping it with the attributes of determinacy.

(p. 12)

Jenkins (1983) also points out that an over-dependence on the term 'subculture' tends to rule out any understanding of the commonalities between subcultural groups. In turn, a determinate and often deviant relationship to a dominant culture is often assumed, resulting in a mis-understanding of youth lifestyles. However, basing his discussion of lifestyles on a Weberian model, Jenkins also insists that lifestyles are derived essentially from class and status. In effect, lifestyles represent the production and reproduction of class in practice. From this point of view the study of youth culture cannot be independent of a study of class which is a, if not *the*, fundamental factor in determining the nature of youth lifestyles. It is worth reinforcing at this point that, unlike 'subculture', the word 'lifestyle' does not imply the domination of young people by dominant orders. It is precisely for this reason that the notion of lifestyles should be prioritized, as it expresses the interplay between structure and agency that operates in young people's daily lives.

Perhaps the only study to present a comprehensive discussion of what constitutes young people's lifestyles is that conducted by Johansson and Miegel (1992). One of their most important points is that youth culture as a resource for youth lifestyles is both conformist *and* creative. It forms part of the broader process of identity construction during which young people become aware of themselves as autonomous cultural beings. Johansson and Miegel point out that lifestyle is at least partly an individual phenomenon that cannot necessarily be defined according to limiting conceptions of group taste, and they argue that lifestyles are 'complex systems consisting of a multitude of relations between individuals' values, attitudes and actions' (p. 292). Young people are in fact very reflective about their lifestyles and readily change them. Indeed, Johansson and Miegel quote one of their respondents, Tor, who points out that 'I change between being the nice guy in blue jeans and a shirt and being a punk rocker. It depends on how I feel' (p. 294). It is therefore the mobility of young people's lifestyles and the way in which such mobility reflects the changing nature of the social world that is fascinating to the sociologist of youth.

Discussion

The sociological understanding of youth lifestyles represents an important means of coming to terms with what it means to be a young person on the threshold of the twenty-first century. This point is well illustrated by Reimer's (1995) research into young people's lifestyles in Sweden in the 1980s and 1990s. Marrying her empirical work with theoretical insights, Reimer argues that the lifestyles of young Swedes have become more active and more entertainment oriented in recent decades. What unites young people as a group is the fact that they simply want to have fun. Indeed, it could be argued that in a world where class relationships are changing, young people are simply more hedonistic than they ever have been before. This is a suggestion I will consider in more detail in Chapter 6. But what is certain, at least in some respects, is that young people's lifestyles are increasingly heterogeneous in a world where more and more leisure opportunities are open to them (see Hendry *et al.* 1993). Although the lifestyle choices that confront young people are as structured now as they ever have been, Reimer argues that the means of expressing those lifestyles have increased and will continue to do so. This reflects broader changes within which sociological conceptions of lifestyle have moved beyond a prepossessing interest in class and status towards a more proactive interest in issues such as ethnicity and gender on the one hand and consumer culture and identity on the other.

To conclude this chapter, it is worth reinforcing the point that young people's lifestyles at the end of the millennium are inherently contradictory: increasingly diverse sources are available to them to construct their lifestyles, and yet these lifestyles appear, at least on the surface, to demonstrate an increasing conservativeness with a small 'c'. It may be that young people are actually more conservative than they were in the past precisely because they no longer appear to have anything to protest against. Calcutt (1998), for example, argues that everybody is alienated and young people do not have anything particularly rebellious to say any more. Young people, are, in effect, looking for self-definition, but have nothing to define themselves against. From this point of view, if the term 'counter-culture' ever existed it is now effectively redundant. Any expression of subversiveness has been transmuted into a commodifiable form. However much young people may believe that they can change the world, their opportunities to do so appear to be very limited; the political world in which they live is apparently a grey, non-committal, insubstantial world which defies definition. In this context, against whom or what can young people possibly define themselves? Calcutt therefore describes the alienated sensibility as the 'new universal'. Ultimately, young people cannot conceive of the world around them improving because

> Unlike fifty years ago, there are no ideologies for today's alienated to define themselves against. Our 'cool' predecessors knew who they were by virtue of the fact that they disbelieved in those singular entities known as Marxism-Leninism and the American/British Way of Life. But nowadays there are no absolute belief systems left to disbelieve in. From priests to politicians, everyone is as pragmatic and pluralist as only rebels without causes used to be.
>
> (Calcutt 1998: 42)

In recent years, sociologists have failed to confront such contradictions largely because of their apparent reluctance to come to terms with the actual life experiences of the people they are studying and with the changing nature of the world which young people inhabit (see Wyn and White 1997). Recent sociological studies of youth seem to have revealed more about the sociologists undertaking the research than about the objects of their study. The task of this book is to illustrate how a focus on youth lifestyles can, potentially at least, begin to reverse this trend. In the next chapter I begin laying the groundwork for this proposition through a discussion of the changing structural conditions which are fundamentally altering the nature of youth lifestyles.

Recommended reading

Chaney, David (1996) *Lifestyles*. London: Routledge.
   A comprehensive discussion of the notion of 'lifestyle' and how it relates to the sociological agenda.
Johansson, T. and Miegel, F. (1992) *Do the Right Thing: Lifestyle and Identity in Contemporary Youth Culture*. Malmo: Graphic Systems.
   Up to now, *the* most authoritative and enlightening empirical discussion of what actually constitutes young people's lifestyles.
Reimer, Bo (1995) Youth and modern lifestyles, in Johan Förnas and Göran Bolin (eds) *Youth Culture in Late Modernity*. London: Sage, pp. 120–44.
   A useful discussion of lifestyles in a Swedish context with particular reference to the work of Pierre Bourdieu.
Sobel, Michael (1981) *Lifestyle and Social Structure: Concepts, Definitions, Analyses*. New York: Academic Press.
   An impressive examination of lifestyles by perhaps the most significant author in the field.

3
STRUCTURES OF YOUTH

Before discussing in detail the changing nature of youth lifestyles and the subsequent implications for the changing nature of the sociology of youth, it is useful to expand on the sorts of practical experiences that characterize young people's lives in a changing world. Although young people's lifestyles represent a key sociological concern, those lifestyles do not emerge entirely independently of social structures. In part, youth lifestyles are a manifestation of the ways in which young people negotiate with structural components of their everyday lives. As I pointed out in Chapter 1, the sociology of youth in recent years has tended to become divided between those commentators who are primarily concerned with structural constraints on young people's lives and those who present a culture-centred approach to young people's lives. One of the concerns that underlies this book is the contention that this divide has served to undermine the development of an effective sociology of youth which will only emerge when cultural aspects of young people's lives are considered in the situated context of structural constraints and vice versa. A tendency for sociologists of youth to specialize in one or other of these areas (and most often, and potentially damagingly, in the former) can only result in a distorted conception of what it is to be a young person. In this chapter, I will therefore outline some of the key structural factors that appear to impinge on young people's lives. This will form the means of constructing a well-contextualized assessment of young people's lifestyles through the book as a whole. The key point to remember is that young people are not entirely free to control the structural influences on their everyday lives as a means of constructing lifestyles in their own image, but neither do these structures completely control who it is young people are. In effect then, young people's lives are an outward expression or negotiation of the relationship between structure and agency.

So what experiences and structural constraints really do affect the construction of young people's everyday lives? What is it like to be a young person at the beginning of the twenty-first century? One of the most useful and accessible treatments of the structural factors that constitute young people's lives can be found in an edition of *Soundings*, a journal of politics and culture. In the introduction to a series of articles on the subject, Jonathon Rutherford (1997) argues that 1990s Britain, in particular, has seen the emergence of an increasingly disadvantaged youth, a small minority of homeless youth symbolizing the way in which the decline in welfare and changes in the job market have appeared to hit young people harder than any other group. Transformations in the nature of capitalism have undermined traditional work-based solidarities which once defined personal identity; as Rutherford (1997) notes, such identities are arguably constructed nowadays by consumption, lifestyles and leisure activities. Although young people live in an increasingly individualized culture, such individualization has been undermined by what Rutherford describes as a massive growth in economic inequality.

These are the sorts of trends described in the mid-1980s by E. Ellis Cashmore in his book *No Future* (1984). Here he identified a situation where working-class young people in particular are simply resigned to an unfulfilling future. In this view, they are perceived as living in a void within which they have few ambitions, limited horizons and minimal prospects. Cashmore paints a depressing picture, despite recognizing that young people are resilient in nature and are capable of at least adapting to this sort of an unfulfilling environment. He does, however, actually conclude on a partially positive note by arguing that the horrendous situation in which some young people found themselves in the 1980s helped breed a new type of resourceful, creative individual capable of surviving on the merest crumbs provided by society. Young people in the 1980s became drifters, masters of boredom and endurance. The question remains: how far did this state of affairs continue into the 1990s and are young people actually more vulnerable now as we enter a new century than they were in the 1980s? Could they be said to be experiencing comparatively worse structural inequalities and dependencies than they have ever done before or have the limitations of the sociology of youth resulted in a situation where the majority of mainstream youth, whose 'transitions' are in fact relatively straightforward, have been neglected by sociologists keen to chart more melodramatic patterns of inequality?

My criticism of the sociology of youth for the way in which it attempts to present an overview of youth inequalities, often based on statistical and questionnaire-based evidence of educational and employment trends, does not mean that this data does not have something to offer. My point is that such an approach has come to characterize what the sociology of youth is all about and, by doing so has presented a potentially misleading picture of what young people are all about. At the heart of young people's experience appears to be the extent to which they can achieve independence, but the achievement of independence is not solely dependent upon the structures determining their destiny, but rather upon how young people negotiate with these structures, often in terms of the everyday construction of their lifestyles. It is in this context that we need to consider what are probably the two main structural influences on young people's lives: education and employment, arenas within which young people are expected to make a whole series of future-forming decisions. The following discussion, though reflecting the structure-oriented nature of the sociology of youth, should provide a basis upon which the significance of youth lifestyles can be more easily contextualized in a way that is more explicitly concerned with the cultural actualities of young people's everyday lives. Recognizing that an overview of young people's experiences will vary considerably from one country to another and that such variation is too complex to chart accurately on a global scale, I will use mainly British illustrations, while referring to the broader picture where it is appropriate to do so.

Education

Education plays a crucial role in young people's lives. Those young people able to take advantage of the best educational opportunities are likely to have an advantage when it comes to taking advantage, in turn, of the often limited opportunities available on the job market. The apparent extension of youth transitions throughout Europe has been accompanied by an increasing pressure on young people to gain qualifications and, in the absence of jobs, a pressure to find something else to do instead (see Adamski and Grootings 1989). What is more, many commentators argue that Britain, in particular, is hampered economically by a less-educated, less-trained and less-skilled workforce than many of its European competitors. While the British government attempts to implement policies aimed at reversing this state of affairs, a situation has been created where young people are simply having to accept the indignity of taking on intermediate statuses (Jones 1995). Instead of accessing the independence generally associated with obtaining their first job, they may have to settle instead for being a trainee or a student. In turn, a global process of 'education inflation' (Côté and Allahar 1996: 124) has resulted in a massive increase in the numbers of young people studying for particular qualifications, thereby undermining the value of those qualifications lower down the scale. Furlong and Cartmel (1997) point out that full-time education among 17- and 18-year-olds in Britain more than doubled between the 1970s and 1990s. On the surface this appears to be a commendable development, but it also represents a reaction to a situation in which employment opportunities are few and far between. This in turn puts considerable pressure on available opportunities. Thus, what has emerged is what Furlong and Cartmel describe as a dual process of standardization and diversification. In other words, young people are spending more years in education and training, building up an improved range of qualifications to equip them for their working lives, while the education experience is itself diversifying in an attempt to meet the needs of this expanding market. As Williamson (1997a) notes, British educational policy during the 1980s and early 1990s was very much ideologically driven and there may well be a case for arguing that that ideology is at least partly a consumer ideology – an ideology that promises the best for every individual but cannot possibly provide it. The classic illustration of the dangers inherent in such an ideologically driven education system is the introduction of 'league tables' on educational performance based purely on examination results. These tables, as Williamson (1997a) points out, do not place relative achievements in the context of socio-economic background. Judgements on the quality of education therefore simply reinforce the inequalities that already exist. Those young people whose socio-economic background puts them at a disadvantage in the first place are made increasingly vulnerable.

Perhaps one of the most significant changes affecting the nature of young people's transitions into adulthood in Britain is the increased governmental emphasis on training. During the 1970s, the vast majority of young people left school at 16 and entered full-time employment. In contrast, Morrow and Richards (1996) point out that in 1996 about a quarter of 16- to 17-year-olds entered training schemes when they left school. The irony here, of course, is that however well trained an individual is, there still may not be a job at the end of such a course. Indeed, as Morrows and Richards indicate, the rate of unemployment among training scheme leavers has gradually increased. Many young people drop out of unsatisfactory training schemes or are not offered jobs at the end of them. As Morrow and Richards (1996: 28) point out: 'The overall conclusion from much of the research on training schemes is that such schemes are too dependent upon employer goodwill, and that the training provided is patchy in quality.' In addition, young people on training schemes are undoubtedly poorly paid, so making the schemes vulnerable to the criticism that they constitute little more than slave labour. For that reason, such schemes (and perhaps most notoriously Youth Training Schemes) became stigmatized in the minds of young people as little more than a last resort should all else fail (see Coles 1995). Above all, as Coles notes, those young people who do take part in youth training schemes are overwhelmingly from working-class backgrounds. The extent to which such training programmes, and those being introduced by the new Labour government in Britain as part of the 'New Deal' initiative, actively address the question of youth unemployment is debatable, and the criticism that such programmes are merely intended to massage the unemployment figures is never far from the surface.

It is important that these changes in the nature of employment are considered in the context of broader social and cultural processes, and that we do not simply dwell on young people as the losers in a zero-sum game they cannot win. This would be far too much of an over-simplification, but it is an over-simplification that tends to pervade the literature. As such, it is briefly worth mentioning the work of Phil Cohen (1997) who relates changes in the education system and in young people's experience of education to the broader political changes associated with Thatcherism and the New Right which had an equally significant impact on the development of educational provision in the United States (see Griffin 1993). In this context, Cohen suggests that children have a special role to play in maintaining a fairy tale propagated by the Conservative government in Britain during the 1980s. This fairy tale convinced us that we could be freed from the shackles of socialism through the joys of an enterprise culture which would in turn reacquaint us with the greatness that by right was Britain's historical inheritance. Cohen argues that education provides the terrain within which this promised land could come about, a vocationalist terrain that would set the British economy on the road to recovery. The essence of this new educational philosophy, according to Cohen, lies in its emphasis on skill-attainment rather than knowledge-attainment, the net result of which was the empowerment of young people as agents of capital rather than labour. Cohen (1997: 287) therefore describes a hidden agenda whereby skills become disassociated from particular practices of manual labour and from any historical association with particular trades or occupational structures:

> Instead work practices are reclassified into 'occupational training families' defined according to a set of purely functional properties of coordination between atomized operations of mind-body-machine interfacing with the same 'information environment'. In this discourse skills have become abstract universal properties of the labour process.

In this respect the training that young people receive in schools, colleges and on training schemes involves an ideological process whereby labour itself is commodified as an interchangeable unit of production. This creates what is supposed to be an increasingly 'flexible' workforce. In fact, that workforce and, in particular, the young people who are propping it up are made increasingly vulnerable to the ups and downs of the economy because their skills are simply not well enough targeted. In an environment within which class arguably continues to impart a major determining role in the construction of work-based destinies, the emphasis on the individual as the author of his or her own career biography plays a proactive role in reshaping people's social aspirations according to the ideological principles of individualism. From this point of view, Thatcherism is all about the creation of an enterprise culture in which individuals become increasingly individualistic so that market values affect every area of social life and individual success arguably appears to become the be all and end all of social life (see Miles 1998).

A skill-based Thatcherite education actively promotes a way of thinking about the world that emphasizes the benefits for self-improvement, while simultaneously shifting young people's perspectives on the world towards a characteristically insular point of view, one in which lifestyle choices come to play a particularly important role. More importantly, as far as education itself is concerned, this process is reflected through the promotion of choice for parents and in particular by the introduction in 1991 of a Parents' Charter which reflected an on-going emphasis on an education system characterized by performance indicators and league tables. The problem here, as Furlong and Cartmel (1997) note, is that consumer choice as represented in the sphere of education tends to mask the inequalities underlying that system. Consumer choice can only ultimately be enacted by those who can afford it. The ideology of individualism and consumer sovereignty can from this point of view be said to amount to little more than a veneer of open access. Changes in education say more about change in how people perceive the world and the role they themselves play in that world, than they do about how the nature of that education itself.

Education clearly plays a fundamental role in influencing young people's career paths and futures throughout the world (see for instance, Adamski and Grootings (1989) for an in-depth discussion of the wider European picture). That such an education is potentially ideological as well as practical clearly alters the very nature of education which appears to be just as much about the shaping of the person in particular ways as it is about the shaping of the worker. But regardless of how young people's opinions about the world may have been altered by global changes in the education system, their actual experience of the work-place, if they are fortunate enough to gain access to it, is of equal impor-tance in shaping their lives, and it is to this issue that I now turn.

Employment

Despite some signs that youth unemployment is improving in many European countries, the 1980s saw youth unemployment rates rise as high as 45 per cent in many EU countries (Popple and Kirby 1997). In Canada, the official unemployment rate for individuals aged 15 to 24 is almost twice the average rate for all groups, while males between the ages of 15 and 19 are likely to have an unemployment rate seven times greater than all individuals aged 25 years or more (Côté and Allahar 1996). Youth unemployment is undoubtedly a global problem (see Touraine 1991).

One of the most useful discussions of youth employment and unem-ployment in contemporary Britain can be found in the work of Ken Roberts (1995) who identifies a radical decline in youth employment in recent years at what is a much faster rate than the rise of general unem-ployment between the 1980s and early 1990s. According to Roberts, young people are exceptionally susceptible to the ups and downs of economic restructuring, most notably in the aftermath of the recession of the early 1980s which itself reflected global changes in the demand for labour to which young people were particularly vulnerable. In this context, Brinkley (1997) describes young people as 'under-worked and under-paid', the problem being that deregulation and the freedom of the market-place have not necessarily benefited young people as much as might have been hoped. Indeed, Brinkley points out that the relative posi-tion of the under 25s in Britain has worsened during the 1990s, with the gap between the unemployment rate for all ages and that of the under 25s being greater in the 1990s than it was in the 1980s. Young people are relatively worse off in terms of employment than the workforce as a whole. In fact, young people make up 35 per cent of the long-term unemployed. Meanwhile, young people appear to be especially susceptible to the mismatch that exists between the sorts of jobs on offer and the sorts of jobs they are actually seeking. The move towards part-time and temporary employment has hit young people particularly badly as they are arguably the most vulnerable sector of the labour force and as such are increasingly having to take up jobs, or 'McJobs', which demand fewer or lower qualifications than they have actually attained. The problem seems to be that youth unemployment is highly sensitive to overall economic conditions. Not only can young people be described as an index of social ills and a barometer of social change, but also as beacons of economic stresses and strains. In this context, Brinkley argues that deregulation simply does not work and that the main source of hope for the future of youth employment lies in the implementation of the minimum wage in 1999. What is clear is that the youth labour market has been radically transformed in recent years; indeed, some commentators go as far as to argue that there is no longer any such thing as a youth labour market (Skilbeck *et al.* 1994; Maguire and Maguire 1997).

Perhaps one of the most concerning aspects of the above developments is that young people are increasingly economically dependent on their parents and that family relationships appear to have changed markedly as a result of this. Indeed, as Rutherford (1997) points out, 64 per cent of 16- to 24-year-olds in Britain live with their parents. Meanwhile, young people have suffered severe cuts to the benefits they are entitled to receive, as the system seeks to shift the responsibility for unemployment onto the moral and personal conduct of the individual. This creates a situation where the pressures on both the family unit and on young people going through a key transitional phase in their lives are compounded.

> The effect is to drive thousands of young people off benefit and out of the mainstream economy altogether, either into an indefinite dependency on their families or into illicit forms of money making. Enforced economic dependency takes away young people's cultural, social and personal autonomy and denies them any semblance of citizenship.
>
> (Rutherford 1997: 120)

Herein lies a key issue. Young people are unable to attain full citizenship in a society that barely knows how to provide them with the opportunities such citizenship entails. Indeed, it might be reasonable to suggest that in many respects young people occupy a state of purgatory between having no rights as children and having full rights as adults. Young people, in effect, are incomplete adults with incomplete rights which can more or less be ignored. In this context, Gill Jones (1995) talks about how young people appear to be caught in what amounts to a state of limbo between dependence and independence. Young people are finding it increasingly difficult to enter the job market, and, having none of the rights of taxpayers, are therefore often unable to take advantage of the benefits available from the welfare state. Jones does, however, acknowledge the introduction of a series of measures that have effectively extended young people's dependency upon their families up until the age of 25, the most notable perhaps being the withdrawal of unemployment benefit for under-18s (Jones 1995). Young people are left to deal with a situation in which securing a viable income is becoming increasingly less likely and in which the safety net beneath them is ridden with bigger and bigger holes. In effect, then, the period of dependency in youth has been extended by an extension of training and education, the shrinkage of the youth labour market and a reduction in state support (Jones 1995: 30). In this context, Touraine (1991) describes a global economic crisis which has created a situation in which the job market actively discriminates against young people and in which young people are forced to conform and adapt.

Status Zer0 youth?

Commentators have used a variety of explanatory notions as a means of coming to terms with the above issues. At this stage I want to focus on just one: discussions of 'Status Zer0' youth. The emergence of 'Status Zer0' youth in Britain – young people in their mid-teens who do not appear to participate in education, training and employment and who are therefore consigned to marginalized economic futures – was identified by Williamson (1997) who based his research on the experiences of young people in south and mid-Glamorgan, the latter being one of the poorest regions in Britain. Although perhaps most insightful when dealing with those young people who are most clearly socially excluded, this notion can also provide an informative angle on some of the problems that young people generally are facing today.

I have already described a situation in which de-industrialization and subsequent structural unemployment have apparently hit young people disproportionately hard, 'obscuring paths to adult statuses, identities and activities' (MacDonald 1997: 186). In other words, young people have been 'lost' in the transition between school and work, with as many as 30,000 young people actively refusing to participate in YTS for example (Williamson 1997a). Williamson identifies a situation where a considerable number of people aged 16 and 17 are not in education, training or employment, despite their being ineligible for income support (Williamson 1997a). Interestingly, Williamson argues that the increase in the numbers of young people electing to continue in education beyond school age is more a reflection of the contracting labour market than it is of any deep-rooted motivation to gain additional skills and qualifications. Such developments illustrate the extent to which young people have been generally disaffected from both youth training and the 'transition infrastructure' (the education system and the careers service, for instance) (Williamson 1997a). Young people are therefore partaking in more informal and often illegal arenas precisely because they feel that more formal structures cannot offer them anything. Williamson estimates that 'Status Zer0' youth constitute anywhere between 16 per cent and 23 per cent of the age group and as such are much more than a small problem – quite possibly they make up the largest single group of each age cohort. These young people's backgrounds are typically 'fractured' in so far as they often experience violence in some form or another, their school attendance is intermittent and homelessness relatively common. But not all 'Status Zer0' young people are the products of an anti-school culture. Many have high educational aspirations, and this, as Williamson (1997) points out, illustrates the potential vulnerability of young people in general. An important issue to recognize, however, is that these young people are united by the belief that the benefits and training system was not serving their needs and that somehow they had to top up their earnings even if that meant (as it did quite often) engaging in criminal activity:

> many [of these young people] were having great difficulty in making sense of their current predicament: they were the victims as much as the shapers of their circumstances. Few gave much thought to the future, since their whole culture and life-styles are about living for the present. It is perhaps wise, psychologically, for them not to contemplate their likely future of unemployment and marginality. Not all, however, had given up hope; many in fact remained surprisingly optimistic that, eventually, things would get better.
>
> (Williamson 1997: 116)

What is interesting in this context is that young people, and in particular those pursuing criminal careers, are dismissive of the support provided by the training system because it simply does not provide them with the resources they need to maintain the sort of lifestyle they want and to which they have become accustomed through the opportunities provided by criminal activities and the escape they found through drug cultures. Crime, in particular, provides a modest income, a way of killing time and a means of avoiding having to contemplate the future (Williamson 1997). More prosaically, Williamson (1997) found that many young people in his research area clearly live their lives from day-to-day and that few, if any, aspects of their lives have any stability. Money and the need to secure a roof over their heads is a constant preoccupation. Young people's lives are therefore characterized by short-term expediency, largely because they simply do not have the opportunities or freedoms to approach life in any other way. Interestingly, Williamson's respondents did not tend to blame themselves for their predicament, but expressed their dissatisfaction that they had been let down by others including parents, politicians and professionals. This much is understandable, although ultimately it might well be argued that the system rather than any individuals within that system has let these young people down. More broadly, as Williamson (1997) argues, the problem with youth policy appears to be that it has tended to impose a vision of what and who young people are without taking into account their cultural and political orientations or those of the communities in which they live.

> To secure a real handle on the experiences and orientations of more alienated young people, one has to engage with them on their own ground . . . If one is truly going to 'engage the user', one has to seize opportunities, 'duck and dive' and jump around in order to obtain data which will provide an authentic illumination of the condition of marginal young people.
>
> (Williamson 1997: 13)

Young people as 'citizens'?

In the above context, Jones and Wallace (1992) echo some of Jones' (1995) sentiments in arguing that the question of citizenship provides a more useful framework in understanding the 'end product' of youth than that of adulthood in the sense that it provides us with more of an insight into the question of inequality and, in particular, the rights of young people. It tends to be assumed that young people will reach adulthood at some stage, regardless of these inequalities. But if young people do not have the necessary resources at their disposal they will not necessarily achieve full citizenship. In this respect, it can be argued that the key factor underlying young people's inequality is economic dependence. In turn, the problem for young people is that citizenship appears, in many ways, to be based on the very thing that young people cannot achieve, namely consumer citizenship. Certainly, young people can consume in all sorts of fashion-orientated ways, but ultimately they are not economically dependent and therefore cannot be fully-fledged citizens of the consumer society that surrounds them. Youth lifestyles provide a particularly effective focus for sociologists of youth in so far as they represent an arena within which ideological aspects of life in a consumer society are actively expressed. Young people may negotiate their place in the job market, they may make strategic personal decisions about their working futures, but they do not necessarily feel entirely in control of those choices. Consumer lifestyles do give them that feeling of control even if it is merely illusory.

It is worth remembering that there is undoubtedly a significant class dimension to the sorts of broad trends I am describing here, but that the significance of that dimension remains hotly debated. Young people from working-class backgrounds are far more likely to suffer from unemployment than their middle-class counterparts, just as they are less likely to get the opportunity to go to better resourced schools. The latter point is a timely reminder that the problems young people experience are not simply youth problems but problems that owe much to the broader spectrum of social inequality which characterizes contemporary British society. This issue is highlighted by Furlong and Cartmel (1997) who describe what they call the 'epistemological fallacy' of late modernity. What they mean by this is that although the experiences of young people have radically altered in recent years, this has not brought with it a loosening of the influence of the key structural factors that underpin young people's experiences of social life. Collectivist traditions such as the support mechanism of the family have been undermined in many ways, but the risks young people are experiencing, according to Furlong and Cartmel, are in fact reinforcing social divisions characteristic of the traditional order such as class and gender. Although Furlong and Cartmel's assumption that a post-Fordist economy does exist is highly debatable, their discussion of the new types of vulnerability that young people are experiencing is an important one. The traditional forms of inequality continue to play an influential role in structuring people's lives. Above all, and despite Williamson's (1997a) contrary argument above, the problems young people experience in gaining employment, for example, become personal in the sense that any failures to do so are perceived by them as being their own fault. As I will point out in Chapter 4, individuals are therefore forced to negotiate a highly risky path through their daily lives and

> yet the intensification of individualism means that crises are perceived as individual shortcomings rather than the outcome of processes

which are largely outside the control of individuals. In this context, we have seen that some of the problems faced by young people in modern Britain stem from an attempt to negotiate difficulties on an individual level. Blind to the existence of powerful chains of inter-dependency, young people frequently attempt to resolve collective problems through individual action and hold themselves responsible for their inevitable failure.

(Furlong and Cartmel 1997: 114)

The challenge for the sociology of youth is to directly address the arenas within which young people address the risks associated with transitions into adulthood. It is one thing to acknowledge that young people blame themselves for structural constraints impinging on their lives, but the next stage is to prioritize the personal negotiation of those structures as a focus for a more flexible and focused sociology of youth. It is simply not enough to describe blandly the patterns of youth employment and unemployment, for the everyday impact on the way in which young people perceive such experiences is just as important a consideration – perhaps more so. In his specific discussion of the underclass thesis, MacDonald (1998) calls for research that focuses on the cultural responses young people deploy when excluded from capitalist production. He suggests that longitudinal ethnographic work looking at 'new cultures of accommodation, resistance and survival amongst the youthful population' (p. 173) might provide the key for the construction of a new agenda for youth research in the United Kingdom and beyond.

Discussion

It is certainly true that a new agenda for youth research is required. The suggestion I am making is that youth lifestyles provide one approach by which this new agenda might be explored. This should help lift the 'transition debate' out of 'the sociological specialism to which . . . [it has] been assigned, and placing . . . [it] more centrally to questions about social change' (Irwin 1995: 312–13). We must at least accept the proposition that employment structures in general have changed, with a decline in manufacturing and a move towards service-based employment. Given this, we must also accept that if there has been any sort of a move towards a post-industrial service economy then young people appear not to have benefited from such change (Hollands 1995). The question remains: why is this the case and how do young people cope with such problems in day-to-day contexts?

This last point is as relevant to young people generally as it is to those who are 'marginal' because in a sense all young people are marginal. The weight of social structure on young people's shoulders does appear to be overwhelming. It may be an unrealistic goal for sociologists of youth to attempt to 'step into the shoes' of young people, but the very least they can do is attempt to address the actual circumstances and contexts within which young people have decided to wear those shoes. It is equally important that sociologists of youth realize there are massive variations in the degree to which young people are disadvantaged and that to portray young people as helpless consumers of structural disadvantage is entirely inappropriate. Middle-class young people, in particular, have all too often been neglected by sociologists of youth. This is one of the reasons why sociologists need to reconsider how best to analyse the sorts of structural constraints I have outlined above. The notion of 'lifestyle' may well provide the most appropriate means of doing this as it taps into the active cultural contexts in which young people establish social relationships. Social structures are intimately related to the cultural contexts in which they are played out, as young people well know. The role of social change is of equal significance. Sociologists of youth 'transitions' forget this at their peril. In the next chapter I discuss those aspects of social change which are of particular relevance to the changing nature of youth lifestyles.

Recommended reading

Adamski, W. and Grootings, P. (eds) (1989) *Youth, Education and Work in Europe*. London: Routledge.
    A somewhat dated, but none the less useful discussion of a Europe-wide research project on young people's relationship with work and education.
Jones, Gill and Wallace, Claire (1992) *Youth, Family and Citizenship*. Buckingham: Open University Press.
    Particularly useful in dealing with the issue of young people as 'citizens'.
Roberts, Ken (1995) *Youth Employment in Modern Britain*. Oxford: Oxford University Press.
    An informative and intelligent discussion of young people's employment patterns with particular reference to questions of individualization.
Williamson, Howard (1997a) *Youth and Policy: Contexts and Consequences*. Aldershot: Ashgate.
    An effective analysis of some of the structural limitations that exist in people's lives with particular reference to the problems experienced by Status Zer0 youth.

4
A CHANGING WORLD

If we accept that some key social and cultural aspects of young people's transitions to adulthood are radically different from what they were in the past, then this has two major implications which demand further contemplation. First, as I discussed in Chapter 1, sociology needs to reconsider the rather outmoded ways of researching young people in favour of a more flexible people-centred approach. Second, if we acknowledge that young people do not exist in a vacuum, but have changed in relation to their everyday social and cultural contexts, then we must consider the social and cultural conditions that have facilitated such change. What is it about an apparently changing world that has provided the preconditions in which young people's lifestyles have apparently been so radically altered? In order to answer this question, I will consider three theoretical themes, each of which has significant implications for the everyday experience of youth: post-modern fragmentation, risk and globalization. I will then proceed to focus on the question of individualization as a means of highlighting how social change has affected the ways in which young people relate both to their peers and to themselves.

Post-modern fragmentation

Sociologists have always been fascinated by the nature of social change, but this fascination has apparently intensified with the emergence in recent years of debates over post-modernity (see Lyon (1994) and Rosenau (1992) for useful overviews). The appeal of post-modernism can partly be explained by the fact that there is no definitive under-standing of what constitutes post-modernity which is itself a highly con-tested term. Broadly speaking, however, approaches to post-modernity can be divided into two main groups: those of commentators who per-ceive contemporary developed societies to be undergoing some form of an epochal shift from modernity to a new phase of post-modernity, and those which see the changes as a continuation of trends that are part of the on-going development of modernity. The first of these two approaches suggests that the world is no longer characterized by the thirst for human progress, but by the acknowledgement that such progress is no longer possible in a world where there is no such thing as reality, but merely representations of reality (see Lash 1990).

From the above point of view, the world is seen as becoming increas-ingly heterogeneous. We apparently live in an eclectic society where post-modern style is emphasized at the expense of substance or content. The sort of social changes involved here are closely associated with the rise of a consumer culture and indeed, globalization, which I will discuss in more detail below. Life becomes little more than a menu from which the individual simply picks and chooses the direction in which he or she wishes to go. Although, it would of course be misleading to imply that there is any such thing as a definitive post-modern position, many post-modern authors argue that society has become a mere mass, that it is no longer composed of individuals or social classes capable of mean-ingful social action. In many respects people are more individual than ever before, but express such individuality through the consumption of mass-produced imagery in a world dominated by surface meaning (see Baudrillard 1988).

In this context, post-modernists such as Baudrillard go as far as to describe the end of the social: the notion that there is no such thing as society, people are rather thrown together in a hotch-potch of styles, opinions and ideas. In this environment people's identities are seen to be increasingly fragmented. In a post-modern world it could be argued that there is no such thing as a sense of self. In fact, many post-modern theorists talk about the 'death of the subject', whereby traditional sources of identity such as the nuclear family, community, and class are seen to be in decline due to the rapidity of social and economic change, while no alternatives emerge to take their place. All that appears to be on offer are the insatiable demands of consumerism or the superficialities of the TV screen, neither of which give an indi-vidual any real sense of personal stability. Taken as an approach to social change in general rather than a school of social theory *per se*, post-modernism reflects the move from a highly rational and rigid society to a highly irrational and flexible pseudo-society which emerged from about the 1960s onwards.

Before I consider the nature of young people's experience of post-modernity, if it indeed exists, it is worth recognizing that many commentators actively debate the extent to which society has undergone an epochal shift. Many, as I suggested above, argue that we are undergoing little more than a continuation of modernity. Frederic Jameson (1984), for instance, sees post-modernity simply as another stage in the development of a capitalist society as is represented by multinational capitalism. Capitalism has emerged as a global totality which has, in turn, transformed our relationship with place and space so that difference has been rejected in favour of sameness. Thus, while on the surface post-modern culture is all about fragmentation and eclecticism, beneath that surface people are consuming the same things in more or less the same ways. A key issue as far as Jameson is concerned is that the production of culture has been integrated into commodity production in general so that post-modernity is essentially hollow and superficial. Jameson therefore identifies a depthless culture which has run out of its own ideas and which is increasingly dependent on mimicking the past in what amounts to a culture of quotations. In other words, social change has taken a profoundly negative turn having somehow lost its innate sense of history.

Interestingly, Wilson (1992) argues that post-modernity represents, in turn, a chaotic culture of contradictions, a culture where capitalism appears to have triumphed, where everybody appears to be better off, alongside a parallel and empty feeling that somehow everything is actually getting worse. This sentiment appears to chime very closely with some of the experiences of young people at the end of the twentieth century. In an increasingly fragmented and material world, which appears to offer more and more opportunities to more and more people, many of those opportunities are blocked by the limitations of under-employment and by the possibility, and perhaps even the probability, of an apparently bleak future. These changes have the potential to impact profoundly on the construction of young people's identities, particularly in respect of their relationship with consumerism. Young people represent the hope for an economically viable future in a post-modern world and as such their relationship with consumerism is highly prized, not only by themselves but by consumer capitalism as a whole. In effect then, consumerism provides a flexible enough arena for the construction of what are inevitably flexible post-modern identities. This promise of flexibility plays on young people's desires for exploration, and above all, for freedom:

> As the consumer market is flexible and more dynamic than the older ways of regulating identities, much more fluidity is apparent: people can change their identities more frequently, experiment with them, select more options from a cultural supermarket with far less commitment than before.
>
> (Harris 1997: 207)

Young people's lifestyles provide the arena within which consumer identities are apparently forged. Whether or not such identities are *forged*, in the sense that they could be perceived as being in some way inauthentic, is another question entirely. When relating debates about post-modernity to the changing experiences of young people there do appear to be some significant points of resonance. Life is entirely about the present and how best to exploit it, regardless of the historical foundations that have made that present possible. In this context, Muggleton (1997) focuses on the changing nature of young people's subcultural experience and goes as far as to describe 'post-subculturalists' who

> no longer have any sense of subcultural 'authenticity', where inception is rooted in particular sociotemporal contexts and tied to underlying social relations . . . This is something that all post-subculturalists are aware of, that there are no rules, that there is no authenticity, no reason for ideological commitment, merely a stylistic game to be played . . . perhaps the very concept of subculture is becoming less applicable in post-modernity, for it maintains its specificity with something to define it against . . .
>
> (pp. 198–9)

Ironically then, young people's experience of the changing world is characterized above all by that world's resistance to acknowledge such change because the change lacks any clear temporal form. Similarly, David Harvey (1989) argues that although in some ways modernity has changed, it is essentially the same in that it reflects the same underlying capitalist dynamic. It is that dynamic that provides a context within which the world appears to be young people's consumerist oyster. However, the reality of social exclusion and extended transitions tends to temper this vision of young people as liberated symbols of post-modern eclecticism, while muddying the definitional waters.

Pointing out that there is no agreed upon conception of what constitutes 'post-modern' youth, Côté and Allahar (1994) consider the key factors that characterize a post-modern world and affect what it is to be a young person. In discussing the work of Tinning and Fitzclarence (1992), Côté and Allahar (1994) argue that the rapid advances made in the development of information technology have had a profound impact on young people whose social lives are increasingly individualized as part of a move towards a globalization of culture. Far from being disadvantaged by these developments young people are empowered in the sense that it gives them a semblance of control over their personal biographies.

But the above is a rather optimistic account of what constitutes young people's lives in a post-modern world. Many commentators prefer to emphasize the fact that post-modernity simply serves to standardize youth experience, or at the other extreme, to rob young people of what unifies them in the first place. Indeed, Best and Kellner (1998) argue that many young people are simply not equipped to cope with the extreme demands of a new high-tech economy because post-modern culture has created a world in which young people are being dumbed down by the mass media (see Chapter 5). From this point of view, young people have been lost in a world of hyper-reality. Using the popular MTV series *Beavis and Butt-Head* as an exemplar of the current state of the teenage life experience, Best and Kellner identify the existence of 'a large teenage underclass that is undereducated; that comes from broken homes; that is angry, resentful, and potentially violent and that has nothing to do but to engage in social mayhem' (p. 88). Focusing in particular on the American example, the authors suggest that a large proportion of young people have been denied a future and as such are almost obliged to choose an alternatively illegal future instead:

> it should be clear that the reality of today's youth is not only the hyperreality of watching TV or surfing the Net, but also difficult lives filled with violence, poverty, homelessness, systematic neglect, drug and alcohol abuse, high pregnancy rates and poor education. They are not merely absorbing images, playing video games, and hanging out at the malls; great numbers of them are suffering, living in fear of various health and safety threats, and under the psychological duress of 'lockdown' from concerned parents aware of the dangers of the streets.
>
> (Best and Kellner 1998: 93)

As Best and Kellner suggest there is a down-side to the ephemerality of post-modernity which clearly has links to the discussion of risk society below. The value of a post-modern approach to social life and to young people more specifically will continue to be hotly debated. The issues raised by the post-modern debate are highly complex and by its very nature such a debate raises more questions than it can ever answer. The post-modern argument that it is simply not possible to conceive of answers to why the world is the way it is, and that we can construct little more than opinions or representations of reality, means that these arguments can never be tested, least of all disproved, because they are not trying to prove anything in the first place. But regardless of such problems, post-modernism has undoubtedly had a profound effect upon the social sciences and at the very least has persuaded sociologists to combine micro and macro interpretations of their subject matter. In other words, post-modernism has recognized the value to be had from studying expressions of culture in their own right, but it does so within a broad debate about the nature of long-term social change and so has the potential to provide insights into the changing nature of youth lifestyles.

To summarize then, the changing nature of the world is actively changing what it is to be a young person at the beginning of a new millennium. The more practical everyday ways in which the nature of youth has apparently been undermined in this context were discussed in Chapter 3. An important part of this debate centres on whether or not this means that youth at the start of the new millennium is in some way a less authentic experience than it has been in the past. This is an issue I will return to throughout this book. All I need to say at this stage is that if young people's experiences of social change have been fragmented and are in that respect different from how they may have been in the past then the actual concepts sociologists use need to be as flexible as the phenomena they are seeking to explain.

Risk society

One of the most important contemporary sociological debates centres upon the question of risk. In some respects, debates about the risk society can be closely related to the sorts of questions posed by post-modernists, the theorists of risk being concerned with the extent to which we can identify the emergence of a new industrial risk society. Indeed, Ulrich Beck prefaces his book, *Risk Society: Towards a New Modernity* (1992), by pointing out that the prefix 'post' is the key word of our times. Many authors have identified risk as a key issue underlying life in the late twentieth century (e.g. Green 1997) with risk assessment permeating all areas of human interest. Furedi (1997) talks about a 'culture of fear' where the struggle to save the world has apparently been surpassed by the need to ensure personal safety. He argues that although people live longer and are healthier and wealthier than they were in the past, these improvements have come at a cost. The social, economic and scientific advances which made these developments possible have actually created new and bigger problems. A distinctly inhuman environment is being created in which people are having to learn to constrain themselves and their actions:

> The virtues held up to be followed are passivity rather than activism, safety rather than boldness. The rather diminished individual that emerges is indulged on the grounds that, in a world awash with conditions and impending catastrophes, he or she is doing a job by just surviving.
>
> (Furedi 1997: 12)

Three authors have had a particular influence on the debate over a 'risk society': Mary Douglas, Ulrich Beck and Anthony Giddens. Mary Douglas (1992) argues that risk and danger are culturally conditioned ideas shaped by the pressures of everyday life. Risk has apparently become central to our social lives precisely because of the move towards a global society. We are liberated from the constraints of local community but at one and the same time are bereft of traditional forms of protection and support mechanisms. Markets play a key role in this process in that they 'suck us (willingly) out of our cosy, dull, local niches and turn us into unencumbered actors, mobile in a world system, but setting us free they leave us exposed. We feel vulnerable' (Douglas 1992: 15). Douglas goes on to suggest that risk fulfils the forensic needs of a new global culture, the shift to a world community having constructed a new set of political priorities. Risk fits the bill in that it provides a neutral vocabulary for the conception of social change. Risk is forward-looking and provides a means of assessing the dangers ahead, while simultaneously serving the needs of what is an increasingly individualistic culture. That is, it provides a discourse within which the individual can look forward to being protected. Thus, discussions about risk, especially as propagated by the media, are not about community but about the protection of the individual. Risk therefore helps to prop up a culture in which the liberty of the individual remains a political priority, not to say a political vote winner. Risk has therefore been politicized precisely because it provides a discourse which promotes the liberty of the individual. This is not a process that has been thrust upon the populace, but one that they gratefully collude in.

Ulrich Beck (1992) perhaps goes further than Douglas in that he sees risk as the defining characteristic of the developed world. For Beck the contemporary world is fundamentally divided not by differentials in access to the production of wealth, but by the distribution of risks (see Green 1997, for a discussion of risk and its role within the social sciences). We no longer live in a safe predictable world, but one that is characterized by uncertainty and risks which, broadly speaking, operate at two levels: the global environmental level and the everyday personal level. Thus, Beck (1992) argues that it is possible to identify a new mode of socialization, a 'metamorphosis' or 'categorical shift' in the make-up of the relationship between the individual and society. He suggests that while society cannot be said to be 'post-modern' as such, it has reached an important stage in its 'evolution' in which it is having to reflect back on itself (see Kumar 1995). This need for reflexivity is characterized above all by the preponderance of risk in contemporary society. Beck conceptualizes the question of risk within a further discussion of reflexive modernization, arguing that modernization is dissolving industrial society and giving rise to another form of modernity. Risk society therefore develops as a means of modernizing the principles of modernity, as Kumar (1995) notes, so that the onus is less on the potential for self-destruction which characterized industrial society and more on modernization. For Beck, in advanced society, the social reproduction of wealth is systematically accompanied by the social production of risks:

> *Risk* may be defined as a *systematic way of dealing with hazards and insecurities induced and introduced by modernization itself.* Risks, as opposed to older dangers, are consequences which relate to the threatening force of modernization and to its globalization of doubt. They are *politically reflexive.*
> (Beck 1992: 21 [emphasis in the original])

In short, a risk society is a far more pessimistic society than its predecessor. It is more about preventing or limiting the impact of the negative aspects of modernization than it is about everybody wanting to get the most out of it as was more characteristic of a class-based industrial society. The pursuit of success through the production of wealth, once the key characteristic of modern society, has been overtaken by the production of risk and the subsequent quest for safety. Modern technology can be seen as playing a major role in creating large-scale risks, most notably the potential for nuclear war and environmental disaster. Of more interest here, however, are those risks associated with what Beck calls 'individualization'. In this context he identifies three main patterns:

1 The increasing focus on the individual as a reproduction unit for the social in his or her life-world. This development has significant implications for the nature of the 'social' and the concomitant decline of traditional forms of social support. Indeed

> the family collapses as the 'penultimate' synthesis of life situations between the generations and the sexes, and individuals inside and outside the family become the agents of their livelihood mediated by the market, as well as of their biographical planning and organization.
>
> > (Beck 1992: 130)

2 A high degree of standardization which accompanies the above. This process is underpinned by the extension of the market into every aspect of social life. Traditional sources of social support are undermined and the individual becomes just as standardized as he or she is individualized (see Simmel (1978) and his analysis of money).

3 A concomitant change in the nature of individual situations so that the individual becomes increasingly, and ironically perhaps, dependent upon institutions. Although liberated on one level, the individual actually becomes increasingly dependent on his or her relationship with the labour market, which is especially ironic for young people who often find it so difficult to gain access to it. The individual is equally dependent on education, consumption, the welfare state, 'and on possibilities and fashions in medical, psychological and pedagogical counselling and care ... Individualization becomes the *most advanced* form of societalization dependent on the market, law, education and so on' (Beck 1992: 130–1).

In this situation, class and family contexts become less important as the individual becomes more responsible for his or her own direction in life. Two people may have very similar backgrounds but are at liberty to choose different lifestyles, subcultures, social ties and identities. And herein lies Beck's fundamental point:

> The individual is indeed removed from traditional commitments and support relationships, but exchanges them for the constraints of existence in the labor market and as a consumer, with the standardizations and controls they contain. The place of *traditional* ties and social forms (social class, nuclear family) is taken by *secondary* agencies and institutions, which stamp the biography of the individual and make that person dependent upon fashions, social

policy, economic cycles and markets, contrary to the image of individual control which establishes itself in consciousness.

(Beck 1992: 131)

The individual's relationship with risk is apparently changing in that the individual has less and less control over those risks that surround him or her, a classic illustration of this being a young person's experience of the employment market. But a key point made by Beck in this context, and one that is often overlooked, is that the process of individualization brings with it market dependency which invades all aspects of living. The mass market and mass consumption come to play a key role in structuring everyday existence notably through the construction of lifestyles 'launched and adopted through the mass media' (Beck 1992: 132). The market therefore plays a key role as an external form of control and standardization. In this context, the individual is institutionally dependent, that dependency being most readily reflected in the peer group's relationship to the labour market. And yet the irony of all this is that individuals perceive their social lives, not as being determined by the social or by social institutions, but as revolving around their own egos. In other words, the individual's biography lies in his or her own hands, this being a necessity in a world with arguably fewer genuine forms of social support than ever before.

Anthony Giddens (1991) is equally concerned with the nature of social change but sees it as part of the long-term evolution of modernity. To this end, Giddens talks about the onset of 'high modernity', one of the key characteristics of which is the uncertainty it manages to engender in the individual. As Green (1997) argues, in a world where scientific explanations are fracturing and where the understanding of what constitutes 'truth' and who is responsible for maintaining such truth becomes increasingly hazy, the individual is forced to respond to what is a rapidly changing and uncertain environment. These are themes that Giddens (1991) develops when he argues that living in high modernity 'has the feeling of riding a juggernaut' (p. 28). High modernity then is simultaneously a time of risk, danger and yet infinite possibility: 'Living in the "risk society" means living with a calculative attitude to the open possibilities of action, positive and negative, with which, as individuals and globally, we are confronted in a continuous way in our contemporary social existence' (Giddens 1991: 28).

For Giddens, the risk society is a society in which the individual is confronted with an infinite range of potential courses of action which themselves breed an atmosphere of self-doubt and anxiety. The point here is not that there is greater insecurity living in a high modern society than there would have been in the past, but that anxieties are generated by the increase in risk calculations which feeds the 'culture of fear'. Giddens recognizes the possibility that individuals can make particular lifestyle choices as a means of minimizing anxiety. But such a strategy, he argues, is limited due to the sheer overwhelming magnitude of life possibilities perceived by the individual on a day-to-day basis. These possibilities are extended by the process of globalization (which I discuss in more detail below) in the sense that global transformations are increasingly tied up with everyday activity and hence the constitution of the self. In high modernity self-identities are intimately bound up with crisis situations thereby making the narrative of self-identity permanently fragile. The world in which we live is markedly different from that of the past. Our local lives are directly affected by and directly express global experiences and this creates a radically different type of social experience.

Two authors who have considered most comprehensively the question of risk and how risk relates specifically to young people's lives are Andy Furlong and Fred Cartmel (1997). They argue that young people have become especially vulnerable to the heightened sense of risk and the individualization of experience which has characterized the move towards 'high modernity'. 'Young people today are growing up in a different world to that experienced by previous generations – changes which are significant enough to merit a reconceptualization of youth transitions and processes of social reproduction' (Furlong and Cartmel 1997: 6).

Furlong and Cartmel go on to suggest that young people are facing a greater diversity of risks and opportunities in the modern world, and with the traditional links between family, work and school breaking down, their journeys into adulthood are becoming increasingly precarious. Moreover,

> because there are a much greater range of pathways to choose from, young people may develop the impression that their own route is unique and that the risks they face are to be overcome as individuals rather than as members of a collectivity.
>
> (Furlong and Cartmel 1997: 7)

Furlong and Cartmel describe a society where the old social cleavages associated with class and gender remain intact, to the extent that objective forms of risk have changed little, while subjective feelings of risk have grown out of all proportion due to a perceived lack of collective tradition and security. In this context, young people's identities are inevitably and increasingly fragile. To back up this proposition, Furlong and Cartmel describe a situation in which patterns of education and employment have changed radically in recent years (see Chapter 3). Transitions into adulthood have therefore been extended, partly reflecting the increased difficulties young people experience in entering the labour market, which in itself makes education an increasingly attractive prospect. This in turn, results in young people being dependent upon their family for longer periods than was previously the case.

What is perhaps most interesting as far as the changing nature of young people's lifestyles is concerned is that family ties have weakened, while other influences on young people's lives – particularly the media and peer groups – have apparently strengthened. Consumption and lifestyles are arguably now central to the process of identity construction. Furlong and Cartmel actually go as far as to suggest that although consumption and style have not succeeded class as the main determinant of young people's lives, consumer lifestyles are actually very stressful in nature and the sense of risk experienced by young people is very much a product of the consumer society. Indeed, in this context it is worth considering the suggestion that young people react to the sorts of inequalities and risks I have outlined above by partaking in increasingly risky types of behaviour themselves. As Plant and Plant (1992) argue, risk-taking behaviour such as drug and alcohol consumption is simply a way in which young people react to the structural conditions which operate around them. In this context, Plant and Plant go on to discuss the work of Jessor *et al.* (1990) who in turn argue that risk-taking by young people is, by definition, entwined with lifestyle. In many respects risk is a product of socially organized poverty, inequality and discrimination.

Globalization

Globalization appears to pervade questions of post-modernity and risk. It has emerged as a key focus for sociological debate in recent years with the recognition that much of what happens in our daily lives is increasingly influenced by events beyond our 'local world' (see Allen and Massey 1995). Anthony Giddens has defined globalization as 'the intensification of worldwide social relations which link distant localities in such a way that local happenings are shaped by events occurring many miles away and vice versa' (Giddens 1991: 64).

If we are to understand the local nature of our lives, including the local expression of youth lifestyles, we have also to consider the global context within which the local operates. In other words, there is a geographical dimension to the sorts of cultural issues under discussion in this book, with a careful balance to be made between global interdependence and local character. We can only understand the changes taking place in our locality if we are prepared to understand changes taking place outside our locality that may directly or indirectly affect the nature of that locality (Allen and Massey 1995: 1).

But globalization is a multidimensional phenomenon. There are, as Allen and Massey suggest, many 'globalizations' including the globalization of telecommunications, of finance and of culture. On the economic level the actions of transnational companies are seen to be central to the globalization of production. Companies no longer make location or investment decisions on a national basis, but consider their options on a global scale. Meanwhile, the world's financial markets are connected through rapid developments in information technology which mean that capital and resources can be switched around the world at the touch of a button. Though the above aspects of globalization are virtually invisible to the individual, the implications of such a process are very real. As more and more companies work on a global basis, crucial decisions can be made about the viability of an individual's job perhaps thousands of miles away. The decision-makers, being remote from the impacts of their policies, are likely to be more hard-headed and less sentimental than if they were making a locally-based decision.

A key development is thus the receding influence of the nation-state – a phenomenon that some authors have described as 'time-space compression' or 'time-space distanciation'. David Harvey (1989), who relates his discussion of time-space compression closely to that of postmodernity, considers the ways in which global capitalism has speeded up in recent decades, resulting in massive disruptions and implications for political-economic practices, the balance of class power, and social and cultural life in general. The acceleration in production and the associated accelerations in exchange and consumption have apparently resulted in an increasingly volatile and ephemeral market which in turn has undermined the stability of youth lifestyles, precisely because young people represent the social group perhaps most likely to partake in ephemeral forms of consumption. Our culture then is increasingly unstable and disposable, for we live in a world where we throw away 'values, lifestyles, stable relationships, and attachments to things, buildings, places, people, and received ways of doing and being' (Harvey 1989: 286). The problem with all this, according to Harvey, is that we may not be able to cope as easily with such rapid social change as well as we might think. Globalization as expressed through time-space compression has created an ever more stressful world.

The sense that the world is simply out of the individual's control is an immensely frightening but common one in the global society. This is an issue taken up by Giddens (1991) in his book *Modernity and Self-Identity* in which he discusses the concept of 'time-space distanciation'. In discussing globalization as a dialectical phenomenon impacting upon divergent events at both a global and a local level, Giddens point out that nobody can 'opt out' of the transformations brought about by modernity. Everybody, for instance, is threatened by nuclear war or ecological catastrophe. But at the individual, day-to-day level, Giddens argues that globalization has an impact on intensional as well as extensional change. The sense of powerlessness which globalization brings with it can have a profound impact upon the self.

Globalization is not then simply an abstract theoretical notion. It actively impinges on people's daily lives. Indeed, as Spybey (1996) suggests, the single most important point about globalization is that it enters directly into the day-to-day reproduction of social institutions. People are socialized in the light of 'global knowledge, global awareness and global images' (p. 151). In illustrating this point, Spybey discusses Giddens' work in some detail and in particular his contention that traditional institutions are 'disembedded' in favour of globalized communication, authorization, allocation and sanction. Thus, Giddens describes the 'duality of structure', the idea that flows of the global are only reproduced in time and time space through human contact in passing moments. But perhaps most important of all here is the debate as to whether or not globalization promotes mass participation on an increasingly global scale while breaking down gaps between the haves and the have-nots. This is clearly not entirely true because, as Spybey suggests, an increasing division in a global culture is between those who are familiar with technological developments and those who are not. Fortunately young people tend to fall into the former category.

In the context of this book, the globalization of culture, and more specifically the globalization of the mass media, is a central concern, as is the suggestion that this process has broken down barriers between different cultures. In other words, there has arguably been a move towards a common global culture sparked off by new technologies of communication (Allen and Massey 1995). On the one hand, this process is seen to transmit a whole range of cross-cultural influences worldwide. On the other, it is seen as potentially damaging to local cultures which are increasingly threatened by external influences and, not least, by American influences. These in turn may result in the standardization and massification of culture on a global scale. Albrow (1997) argues that it may even be possible to talk about the end of culture, in the sense that the massification of global culture through the particularity of mega-stars and global media events and images has created a situation where culture is no longer simply about the historic experience of a people. In other words, the whole concept of culture has been disembedded from its territorial base 'and re-embedded in a mass communications media frame' (Albrow 1997: 29). The problem with this situation, as I will discuss further in Chapter 5, is that American culture and culture portrayed by the media (particularly satellite television) presents a very particular image of the world:

> The message on the radio or television which speaks across linguistic and cultural communities is that they too can also gain access to the consumer trappings of the advanced economies; if they have not already started to do so in the shape of a pair of Nike trainers or a Ford motor car or pick-up.
>
> (Allen and Massey 1995: 114)

In this context, Street's (1997) discussion of global popular culture is of particular interest. Street points out that the rhetoric of global culture has been detached from the material and institutional conditions that underlie the appearance of globalization. In particular, globalization is not constituted by a plurality of cultures intermingling or by a harmonious synthesis of a single global culture but by a struggle for power. Power operates at two levels in this context. American culture may be a global heavyweight compared with that, say, of Honduras, but American culture may actually be received in a very different way in Honduras than it is in the United States. Honduras may not have the global cultural influence of the United States but at least it can interpret popular culture wherever it may emanate from, in the way it sees fit. Furthermore, it should not be assumed that popular culture is truly global: access to global American culture in remote parts of Honduras will clearly be much more restricted than in down-town San Francisco, for example. In this respect, globalization is clearly political as well as cultural, and part of the political impact of globalization relates in turn to the question of homogenization.

Waters (1995) develops these arguments with a discussion of the homogenizing impact of a global consumer culture which may have particular implications for young people's lives. But such 'homogenisations' are not entirely straightforward. Certainly, what is available in any single locality can be available in all localities, but in any particular locality cultural opportunities can also be widened. The concern here is that this process actually conflates the individual's identity *to* culture. However, as Billington *et al.* (1998) point out, it should not necessarily be assumed that patterns of consumption simply follow some kind of global script. Consumers can appropriate mass consumer goods and use them to their own ends, as Billington *et al.* (1998) and Friedman (1990) have shown in their discussion of consumption in the People's Republic of Congo. Friedman identifies specific ways in which young men in the Congo, who belong to a low-status social group known as the *sape*, create high status identities through the consumption of global goods. They wear designer goods with ostentatious designer names, while displaying cans of global soft drinks in their cars. Such actions are not simply symptomatic of a third world country desperate to ape its first world 'masters'. What matters to these people is that these products provide an immediate means by which they can establish their own forms of social power. According to Friedman, the purchase of designer clothes in the West is a way of infiltrating a higher social order; the third world is all about assaulting and undermining dominant social orders. In other words, from our skewed Western viewpoints it is also too easy to make crass generalizations about the nature of globalization when in actual fact local identity is 'constituted through face-to-face relationships that occur in social contexts where there is little territorial movement' (Billington *et al.* 1998: 298). Nevertheless, in discussing the work of Hannerz (1992), Billington *et al.* point out that cultures can just as easily be located in collective structures of meaning that transcend space as they can be territorial:

> Western fashion clothes, trends in travel and tourism, and 'foreign' food are now available throughout the world. Yet, when individuals use them or consume them they do not seem to become 'global villagers'. Instead, such items take on meanings that are specific to the individual's local context. They become part of the social repertoire through which individuals and groups assert *particular* ethnic, gender or class-based identities. However, what cannot be overlooked are the external pressures that influence negotiations over power and status which take place at a local level. Thus a global setting of extreme, political, social and economic inequality must be recognised as the wider context.
>
> (Billington *et al.* 1998: 214–15)

The external pressures towards the construction of a common global culture are in this sense enormous, as is, at least potentially, the impact upon the individual's identity. But perhaps the key point here with regard to young people, and in particular the onus society places on them as fledgling consumers, is that globalization and the companies that perpetuate it are dragged towards the production of the ephemeral:

In order to elbow their way through the dense and the dark, strag-
gly, 'deregulated' thicket of global competitiveness and into the
limelight of public attention – goods, services and signals must
arouse desire and in order to do so they must seduce their prospec-
tive consumers and out-seduce their competitors. But once they
have done it they must make room, and quickly, for other objects
of desire, lest the global chase of profit and ever greater profit shall
grind to a halt.

(Bauman 1998: 78)

It could be argued that regardless of either the positive or negative
implications of consumerism, capitalism appears to direct people, and
young people in particular, down a route in which consumer goods and
services become the primary resource for the construction of their identities. Young people represent a prime target for the consumption of
ephemerality, for the consumption of lifestyles. The point is that globalization has played its part in perpetuating consumption as a prime focus
for the construction of lifestyles. Globalization promotes consumerism
because both are temporal and consumers' desires are never quite fulfilled. Thus, the global consumer is constantly looking for promised
unprecedented sensations: 'Consumers are first and foremost gatherers
of sensations; they are collectors of things only in a secondary and derivative sense' (Bauman 1998: 83). If we take Bauman's argument one step
further, young people are clearly the ultimate travelling consumer, intent
on consuming sensation, not only for the sensation itself but for the sensation the sensation creates, as a means of firming up that individual's
identity through desirous day-dreaming (Campbell 1987: ch. 7). More
than any other social group, young consumers actually *want* to be
seduced. Thus, as Côté and Allahar suggest, in the contemporary world
youth cultures do not simply emerge as a result of the actions of marginalized youth but as a result of the impact of modern information
technologies spread by consumer capitalism which has profound implications for the everyday experience of consumerism – with the mass
media playing a fundamental role in this process (see Chapter 5). Some
authors argue that the possibilities provided for young people via consumer capitalism actually liberate them by allowing them to be the
authors of their own biographies. 'As consumers of images and commodities, they can accept or reject these things depending on whether or
not they suit "their life projects" of "self-making"' (Côté and Allahar
1996: 22–3). But ultimately, such self-making, at least on the surface,
appears to be based on the principles of self-gratification.

The suggestion here is not that young people are dupes of global consumer capitalism but that the major impact of globalization on their lives is both economic and cultural. First, young people, perhaps more than any other social group, are subject to the imperatives of global economic change. Second, young people are far more subject to the imperatives of a global culture than any previous generation and as such appear to be virtually obliged to construct global and largely consumption-based lifestyles. Such lifestyles serve to offset the pitfalls associated with the sort of risky post-modern world of uncertainty which they inhabit. In particular as consumers of global culture young people are, by definition, consumers of *cultures*. Their lifestyles provide an arena within which those cultures can be actively negotiated in a process of mutual self-affirmation.

Discussion

The key change touched upon in all three of the above debates, and one that relates closely to the individual's relationship to social change, is individualization. As individuals become increasingly independent and arguably free, the way in which their identity is constructed and the individualized nature of their lifestyles become increasingly interesting to the sociologist. However, as Johansson and Miegel (1992) point out, discussions over individualization should not tempt the sociologist into over-exaggerating the amount of freedom people, and in this case young people, actually have.

> It is probably true that in modern society the individual has gained greater freedom to choose and create her or his specific lifestyle. This is not to say, however, that structure and position no longer play a significant role in the making of lifestyle . . . in modern society neither structure, position, nor the individual, is the sole determinant of lifestyles. Modern lifestyles are the result of a complex interplay between phenomena at all three of these levels.
>
> (Johansson and Miegel 1992: 37–8)

In order to bring the above discussion to a satisfactory close one might ask how the impact of risk, globalization and the move to 'postmodernity' can be related to the construction of youth lifestyles. It is all well and good to point out that the world is changing and that young people are changing with it, but what form does the link between the young people and social change actually take? Two authors who have directly addressed this question are Fornäs and Bolin (1992) in their edited collection, *Moves in Modernity*. Here they point out that modernity appears to be dissolving the traditional distribution of roles so that it is no longer possible to assume that young people are transgressors and reactionaries. In other words, young people are more complex than many conventional and traditional approaches actually allow. Indeed, young people may have a role to play in setting limits and reining in changes as well as perpetuating them. The problem with the sociology of youth in general, as I hinted in Chapter 1, and as Fornäs and Bolin also argue, is that at times it gets so carried away with relating youth to broader socio-cultural trends that the actual object of study, namely young people, gets lost. As a result, the sociology of youth loses any impact in its own right. Of more immediate concern, however, and an issue touched upon by all three discourses discussed above, is that of individualization. As Fornäs and Bolin point out, this concept should not be confused with that of individualism, which implies that everyone is egoistic, or canonizes their own individuality. Instead, Fornäs and Bolin identify a process whereby individuals have increasingly been freed from collective constraints: 'In recent youth culture, there are lots of examples of new constructions of collectivities through mass media, leisure activities or social movements, but these are to a higher degree individually chosen rather than organically grown' (p. 9).

The move towards individualization is also picked up by Michael Mitterauer (1992) who argues that young people's rooms constitute an increasingly significant arena for individuated space (see Steele and Brown 1995). It is in this respect that the territorial youth groups with which sociology has traditionally been fascinated are actually less significant then they were in the past (assuming they were indeed ever 'significant'). In this sense, and as a reflection of broader social change, young people's collectivities tend to be increasingly informal in nature and in turn, their loyalty to a particular territorial focal point is being undermined (although Mitterauer (1992) sees this as more the case for young men than for young women). As far as long-term historical change is concerned, this reflects the emergence of the car and the subsequent 'loss of the street' in favour of a withdrawal into the domestic sphere. The global media appear to have played a particularly influential role in de-territorializing youth and in actively constructing global expressions of musical and fashion-based style. Young people are less dependent on the immediate expression of style in local contexts, because such styles were constantly reaffirmed anyway through the power of the global media.

Interestingly, Mitterauer suggests that the youth experience today is less ritualized than it was in the past. Youth groups are less dependent upon rituals (such as ritual admission via oaths or communal eating) than they used to be. As I argue in Chapter 8, young people's peer relationships undercut their experience of broader social change. However, I would also agree with Mitterauer that the nature of peer relationships, though perhaps equally as significant, have taken on a new guise in which personal relationships are more important than communal ones. A concomitant trend, according to Mitterauer is the de-differentiation of gender roles, with same age and mixed gender groups becoming more and more prevalent. Mitterauer provides a useful example of this development when he discusses the changing nature of young people's relationship with dance. As part of the 'Rock 'n' Roll' ritual for instance, men asked women to dance and led their partner through that dance. New dance styles do not distinguish between an active and a passive partner and therefore individualize the whole experience. There are, of course, exceptions to this process (for example, attendance at football matches) but even these examples are arguably less gender-specific than they have been in the past. The key point is that young people's experiences have been fragmented to the extent that youth groups are gradually losing their function. Young people have common interests which help to frame their communication, 'but they also provide a chance for individual participation without intensive communication' (Mitterauer 1992: 45). Closely bound up with processes of urbanization, young people's lifestyles are not dependent upon a single uniting group to the extent that 'a freedom of choices seems to increasingly be the rule' (Mitterauer 1992: 4). From this perspective young people have more control over their own lifestyles than they had in the past. They are no longer obliged to do what a particular group is doing but can legitimately choose to do their own thing, hence the increasing significance of young people's own space. As Mitterauer (1992: 48) explains, 'the process of individualization, witnessed generally within society, determined the described development from the informal to the territorial group as well as the basic opportunity to do without forming a group at all'.

In summary, the picture of young people that we gain from these discussions is one of increased independence, self-determination and self-realization. But as discussions of risk illustrate, the conditions within which these apparently positive developments are occurring are actually taking place in a world which in some respects is quite possibly less secure than it has ever been. Young people do not have the sort of support from the more formal youth groups (and indeed subcultures) that they may once have had, which in itself leaves them increasingly isolated, and such isolation opens them up to the psychological pitfalls of individualization and self-blame. The changing world in which young people live is a paradoxical one that appears to offer so much, and yet insists on leaving young people on the edge, unsure of whether or not they will ever be in a position to take advantage of the riches associated with a consumer culture. For this reason the mass media plays a particularly significant role in young people's lives as a resource from which they can structure their lifestyles or at least from which they can construct opinions about what lifestyles might be *deemed* to be appropriate.

Recommended reading

Allen, John and Massey, Doreen (1995) *Geographical Worlds*. Oxford: Oxford University Press.
Perhaps the most informative discussion of globalization, particularly its cultural impact.
Beck, Ulrich (1992) *Risk Society: Towards a New Modernity*. London: Sage.
The most important single book to be published on the question of risk and its relationship to social change.
Côté, James, E. and Allahar, Anton, L. (1996) *Generation on Hold: Coming of Age in the Late Twentieth Century*. London: New York University Press.
Particularly useful in coming to terms with the nature of 'post-modern' youth.
Furlong, Andy and Cartmel, Fred (1997) *Young People and Social Change*. Buckingham: Open University Press.
A well-structured and well-argued attempt to relate those structures influencing young people's 'transitions' to how young people experience a 'risk' society.
Lyon, David (1994) *Postmodernity*. Buckingham: Open University Press.
A useful and understandable summary of a highly complex field. The chapter on consumerism is especially informative.

5
YOUTH AND THE MEDIA

One of the most omnipresent and apparently significant arenas in which young people appear to construct or at least interpret their lifestyles in an increasingly individualized world is the mass media. However, the extent to which young people can actively endow the mass media with their own meanings is highly debatable and remains a bone of contention among sociologists. In this chapter I will discuss sociological conceptions of young people's relationship with the media before concluding how far that relationship actually determines or even controls the nature of their lifestyles, most notably in a global context. Can young people shape the mass media in their own image or are youth lifestyles simply the product of an all-powerful global capitalist system that actively determines the nature of young people's experience?

Before considering the way in which the mass media impacts upon young people's lives, it is useful to examine briefly the image that the media itself has of young people. The media actively reinforces the idea that 'youth' represents a distinct and important phase in a person's life. The paradox here is that young people appear to be represented by the mass media at one and the same time as symbols and victims of society, as well as a threat to it (see Wyn and White 1997). In his discussion of youth, the media and moral panics, Boëthius (1995) suggests that popular culture as represented in the mass media has always been considered a threat to young people and this threat has itself been expressed most clearly through 'moral panics' – a process by which the mass media exaggerates the deviant or criminal behaviour of young people, often for its own gain. This relates to a wider concern that actual anxieties about social change are strongly linked to how the wider society relates to young people, and that young people, in being more exposed than other social groups to the influences of the mass media, may be more susceptible to its corrupting effects. And yet, it can also be argued that because the mass media is so important to young people, they are exceptionally sophisticated in using it.

The question preoccupying this chapter therefore centres on who is the more powerful partner in the relationship between young people and the mass media. Wyn and White (1997) have argued that young people are not simply represented by the mass media but actively construct the experience and meaning of youth and, as such, are effectively 'offering a frame of reference that may replace traditional frameworks' (p. 20). The mass media often describes young people as a 'problem', and by doing so increases the public perception that they are 'troublesome' and liable to succumb to the excesses of drug and alcohol dependency and, of course, violence. Indeed, as far as Osgerby (1998a) is concerned, media portrayals of young people actually worsened in the 1980s and 1990s as images of youth were increasingly associated with urban and moral decay. This was perhaps expressed most forcibly, in the United Kingdom, by media reaction to the post-Ecstasy death of Leah Betts. However, some commentators point out that young people, being increasingly sophisticated, have become immune to media-driven conceptions of them as 'folk devils' and are instead using the mass media to their own ends. Young people are therefore able to present a more positive image of themselves through fanzines, style magazines and youth TV (McRobbie 1993).

Relating the broader theme of young people's use of the media to associated concerns about young people's consumer lifestyles, Osgerby (1998b) contends that during the economic boom of the 1980s young people were rarely portrayed as symbols of 'consumer empowerment'. This reflected a sea change in the way in which young people were being perceived and represented, the mass media being more concerned with particular mind-sets or lifestyles than with any particular generational qualities which could be pigeon-holed as 'youth'. Hence, the suggestion that youth television no longer exists in its own right but pervades the entire televisual spectrum. Indeed, 'media representations of "youth" are now characterized not by generational age but by a particular lifestyle. "Youth" has become simply a mode of consumption' (Osgerby 1998b: 322), another market niche that needs to be exploited. I will return to this suggestion at the end of this chapter, but before I do so I want to consider the contexts within which commentators have debated young people's use of and relationship with the media.

Media 'effects'

There is an overwhelming number of works addressing the role played by the mass media in young people's lives. Here I will attempt to provide just a flavour of these discussions. One such collection of works is *Media Effects and Beyond: Culture, Socialization and Lifestyles* edited by Karl Erik Rosengren (1994), which presents an overview of a systematic pro-gramme of longitudinal research looking at the causes and consequences of media use among Swedish children and young people. In an article in this collection, Johnsson-Smaragdi (1994) points out that the media fare consumed by young people has radically expanded in recent years, allowing them to compose their own 'media menu' with their own pref-erences and likings. Not only is youth itself undergoing a period of rapid change, but so are the ways in which young people use that media. As far as the middle and late teenage years are concerned, television watch-ing is actually reduced during this period in favour of music listening, and this despite Johnsson-Smaragdi's observation that the advent of cable and satellite television has boosted television viewing in recent years. Generally speaking however, young people do tend to adjust the way they consume the media away from home-oriented media such as the television and books and towards more peer-oriented media such as music and videos. The important point emerging out of Johnsson-Smaragdi's article is that media use is essentially *adaptive*. There are many forces influencing a young person's choice of media; perhaps the most important is the pressure to adhere to certain lifestyles within par-ticular subgroups.

The impact of the media in and on young people's lives is broadly considered within what is referred to as the 'media effects' debate which tends to focus on the potentially negative impact of the media on young people's lives: video violence, gambling, educational performance, mass consumerism and so on. Steele and Brown (1995) identify three main reasons why the media's influence needs to be considered with some circumspection:

1 Young people spend more time with the mass media than they do in school or with their parents.
2 The media are full of portrayals that glamorize risky adult behaviour such as excessive drinking and sexual promiscuity.

3 Parents and other socialization agents have arguably shirked their responsibilities when it comes to directing youth away from risky forms of behaviour; thereby allowing the media a more fundamental influence.

In this context, many commentators have noted that by the age of eighteen an individual will have spent more time engaged in watching television than any other single activity besides sleep (Miles and Anderson 1999). And yet, though it is widely assumed that young people are affected more directly and negatively by the media than any other age group, research actually indicates that young people between the ages of 14 and 24 actually form one of the groups who currently spend the *least* time watching television. This is a paradox that has often been neglected in the literature. Ironically, the mass media itself has a vested interest in exaggerating the impact it has on young people's lives, because media-hype simply makes good 'copy'. The aim of this chapter overall is therefore to present a more rounded discussion of young people's relationship with the media and the role that relationship plays in the construction of youth lifestyles.

Given that people's relationship with the media is constantly being revised, it is worth considering briefly the ways in which children and young people actively *interact* with the mass media. As Buckingham (1997) suggests, the majority of debates about media effects are focused on the child, and, more often than not are inclined to paint a somewhat derogatory picture of children's relationship with the media. For this reason, an understanding of young people's consumption of the media relies on understanding that of children:

> Children are seen here, not as confident adventurers in an age of new challenges and possibilities, but as passive victims of media manipulation; and the media not as potential agents of enlightenment or of democratic citizenship, but as causes of moral degradation and social decline. Children, it would seem, are unable to help themselves; and it is our responsibility as adults to prevent them from gaining access to that which would harm and corrupt them.
>
> (Buckingham 1997: 32)

The classic 'media effects' scenario is that of a child encouraged by the media to commit acts of violence while the media itself commits violence against children in the name of financial greed. Dubow and Miller (1996) claim that laboratory and field investigations have at least proven that television violence viewing is a socially significant influence in encouraging aggressive behaviour among young people.

The problem with this sort of analysis is that it conceives of children and young people alike as somehow lacking the experience and intellectual capacity to deal with the media and interact with it effectively. Realizing this, commentators have recently begun to move away from the sort of approach that sees consumers of the media as an undifferentiated mass in favour of an approach that recognizes that all sorts of variables operate between the media and its consumers. Viewers of television, for example, respond in different ways to the same messages. Thus, as Buckingham (1997) and Young (1990) acknowledge, children and young people alike are far from simply passive consumers of television advertising but view it in a critical and considered fashion. Children and young people, are in effect, active interpreters of meaning. They do not passively receive television meanings, but construct them for themselves. Similarly, use and gratifications research, which tends to see individuals as using the media to satisfy psychological needs, as Buckingham (1997) points out, works on the principle that different children can occupy different 'media worlds' depending on factors such as age, gender and class. How the individual consumer relates to other influences on his or her life and how these in turn affect that individual's media consumption are key considerations. Approaches within cultural studies have also emphasized the social contexts within which children and young people consume the media as active producers of meaning, and the way in which children negotiate their social identities through talk about the media.

As one of the most significant commentators in the field, David Buckingham (1993) extends this debate as far as young people in his edited collection, *Reading Audiences: Young People and the Media*. In the introduction, Buckingham points out that adolescence is generally seen as a very precarious period in a young person's life. Young people are often portrayed as being on the verge of a collapse into primitive abandon, while the media and more specifically the cinema and music have had a major influence on this process. For Buckingham this approach is clearly far too simplistic, as is the suggestion that young people blindly accept celebrations of consumerism inherent in television advertising. The problem arises, according to Buckingham, when commentators discuss the growth of consumerism, for instance, but do so in relation to a single isolated 'cause', with the result that the impact of advertising aimed at young people gets blown out of all proportion. In other words, the media become a scapegoat for the broader woes of society, when such woes are far more complex than such simplistic explanations can ever account for. Buckingham (1993) suggests that the crucial point is that the media are not seen simply as a powerful source of dominant ideologies but as a symbolic resource which young people use to make sense of their everyday lives. Willis' (1990) work on young people's active negotiation of culture as lived practice is equally important in this respect. Willis argues that an individual's identity flows from symbolic exchange out of which social actors emerge. Young consumers of the media do not act passively or uncritically but transform, appropriate and recontextualize meanings. In this context, Wood (1993) agrees with Willis' (1990) assessment that young people's use of the cultural media is characterized by 'symbolic creativity' and that research has generally struggled to come to terms with this creativity. Because of this, such creativity is in danger itself of being exaggerated (Buckingham 1993).

> As in so many other areas of media research, young people have become a focus of forms of concern and debate which often seem to bear little relation to the concrete realities of our lives, or to take account of their perspectives on the issues.
>
> (Wood 1993: 199–200)

The meaning of MTV

Regardless of the actual time young people spend watching television and using the media, there can surely be no doubt that the mass media *have* played and continue to play an important role in structuring young people's lives in some shape or form in a period of rapid social change. Osgerby (1998) points out that the post-modern age brought with it a proliferation of media and information technologies which were challenging traditional conceptions of time and space, symbolized, most powerfully perhaps, by the global cultural flows and images evident in the output of MTV. Auderheide (1986) describes MTV as offering not simply videos, but environment and mood. MTV can therefore arguably be described as an ideal medium by which the instabilities of young people can be harnessed in a youth-friendly environment. MTV, according to Auderheide, is characterized by mutability and the appeal that mutability has for young people who are in an equally mutable state:

> The goal of MTV executive Bob Pittman, the man who designed the channel, is simple: his job, he says, is to 'amplify the mood and include MTV in the mood.' Young Americans, he argues, are 'television babies,' particularly attracted to appeals to heart rather than head. 'If you can get their emotions going,' he says, 'forget their

logic, you've got 'em' . . . Music videos invent the world they represent. And people whose 'natural' universe is that of shopping malls are eager to participate in the process. Watching music videos may be diverting, but the process that music videos embody, echo, and encourage – the constant re-creation of an unstable self – is a full-time job.

(Auderheide 1986: 118–35)

Interestingly, Auderheide suggests that MTV offers young people an alternative into which they can escape. This reflects Rushkoff's (1997) contention that MTV, which might be described as symbolic of young people's media use in general, is more about the texture of its programming than its content, more about style than substance. In a sense then, MTV depends on its viewers being fluent in a particular kind of media language – and young people are the group most conducive to the rough disjointed mediascape that MTV provides. It is not so much that young people are vulnerable to the post-modern excesses of MTV, but that they appear, at least to an extent, to have moulded MTV in their own image. Meanwhile, the impact of MTV has been such that many other aspects of the media have been 'MTV'd' or in effect, 'youthed'. Rushkoff goes as far as to argue that the media have in fact evolved from a top-down incarnation into an interactive free-for-all. According to Rushkoff, young people who are constantly criticized for their short attention spans are in fact sophisticated consumers of the media. The ability to piece together meaning from a discontinuous set of images is actually an important skill from which adults could well learn. Young people may have shorter attention spans than they might have had in the past, but they also have broader attention *ranges*. Young people process images very quickly allowing them to cope more easily with the information overload which characterizes contemporary society. Rushkoff's image of young people's experience of the media is therefore very much an interactive one, symbolized above all perhaps by their increasing participation in the World Wide Web: 'On-line participants wander the global mediaspace like gypsies, gathering and sharing information as individuals, unassociated with institutional authority' (Rushkoff 1997: 189–90).

In trying to sum up the 'media effects' debate and the role of MTV, it is important to recognize that neither end of the debate can explain young people's consumption of the media (see Buckingham 1997). At one end we have an approach that is unrepentant in its insistence that children and young people are active interpreters of the media and so over-romanticizes an image of street-wise sophisticated children; at the other end we have an approach that stubbornly refuses to see young people as anything more than controlled by the media. Both approaches are actively misleading. As a result, the debate is polarized when in fact the truth probably lies somewhere in between. In other words, it should not be assumed that children, or young people for that matter, are active critical consumers of the media. The degree of such activity depends upon the critical resources available to them as regards educational and family influences. On the other hand, however, if the images being portrayed by the mass media operate within a consumerist discourse then that discourse will inevitably play some role in young people's lives precisely because it is appears to be so omnipresent.

Young people and electronic media

In examining young people's use of the mass media, a deeper discussion of the consumption of electronic media in general is potentially revealing, not least because it represents an arena which young people appear to have colonized for themselves. Certainly, many young people exhibit a greater knowledge of the electronic media than their parents. But how do young people actually use electronic media? A popular commonsense argument would be that young people are easily addicted to computer games which in turn prevent them from pursuing more 'worthwhile' and 'fulfilling' pursuits. Kubey (1996) argues that young people are in a sense programmed by computer games in that they react to the constant challenge of harnessing their abilities in the pursuit of victory. Yet in these circumstances young people can never actually fulfil such a need in a constant cycle of game playing within which there is always another level or target to be attained. In this context, Green *et al.* (1998) talk about 'the Nintendo generation' and the way in which children and young people appear to have fallen in love with the computer. They feel that computers are 'theirs', that computers belong, in effect, to their generation. But the worry is that computer games, in particular, are addictive, and that this addiction has some role to play in constructing young people's identities; that somehow the imaginary world of rich signifiers which is projected into young people's front rooms every day on TV is exaggerated by the parallel projection of computer imagery, which creates a world even more imaginary (and, by implication, more dangerous) than the former. Thus, Green *et al.* quote Kinder (1991) who describes video games as 'the first digital technology socialising a generation on a mass scale, worldwide – the vast majority of game players are aged 12–17' (p. 22). Alloway and Gilbert (1998) therefore suggest that young people of this age actively live out the sorts of post-modern subjectivities discussed in the previous chapter. Young people are naturalized into the sort of image-laden world that post-modernists describe and this environment effectively provides the mass media as a resource, a foundation upon which they can conduct their everyday lives. What is interesting about this argument in the context of youth lifestyles is that what lies at its core is the commercial imperative. Indeed, Green *et al.* (1998) quote Kinder again who illustrates this point quite well, 'This process of reproducing the postmodernist subject and its dynamic of commercial empowerment is now being intensified and accelerated in home video games, in commercial transmedia supersystems . . . and in multinational corporate mergers' (p. 38).

Green *et al.* therefore point out that the 'Nintendo generation' is not only computer literate but is an audience of a very particular *market*. The mere reference to the Nintendo generation is symbolic of the power of marketing and advertising in young people's worlds, especially in relation to their consumption of the mass media. Far from the Nintendo generation constructing itself from within, it is clearly, at least to some extent, the product of global consumer capitalism. However, it is equally important to recognize that just because big business has a fundamental role to play in constructing young people's media-driven lifestyles, those same young people cannot actively construct their own cultures within those confines. Indeed, it would not be an exaggeration to suggest that this sentiment underlies the whole ethos of this book.

Despite the potentially liberating role of young people's consumption of the electronic media it is also worth noting that some members of the Nintendo generation are more in control than others. The gender dimension of this equation is especially significant as an indicator of how the consumption of media lifestyles through the mass media benefits some young people at the expense of their peers. Sara McNamee (1998), for example, discusses the relationship between youth, gender and video games, and considers why young women appear to have been excluded from analyses of youth culture and from discussions of media-use in particular. Her research indicated that young women like to play computer games as much as young men and yet have far less access to such games. McNamee suggests that this discrepancy is due to the fact that these young women's brothers have control over access to computers and video games. Bearing in mind the processes of individualization, with male youth cultures moving from the street into the home, it appears that young men have more physical control over space in the home than their female counterparts. This is ironic as, according to McNamee, it reflects a parallel trend in which young women are less easily able to use domestic space as a resistance to young men's supposed domination of the streets. Playing with computer games is therefore not a straightforward matter of choice for girls and young women because access to the world of Nintendo is constrained. Computers and video games are in themselves imbued with gender power relations as are young people's lifestyles in general.

However, Rushkoff (1997) makes the interesting point that young people are perhaps best equipped to cope with the changes he describes as constituting the transition from an information age to the age of chaos. As 'natives' of chaos, the forms of popular culture that young people engage with have effectively prepared them for the social changes that surround them. Thus, Rushkoff describes a generation of 'screenagers', young people born into a world mediated by the television and computers who could teach adults an awful lot about how to adapt in a post-modern world. 'Kids are our test sample. They are, already, the thing that we must become' (Rushkoff 1997: 13). In particular, adults are fearful of the fragmentation characteristic of a global culture, whereas young people embrace such fragmentation and the media technologies that promote it. In this respect, whatever ideological role the mass media may or may not be playing, it is still essential in relating young people to the ups and downs of social change.

Mediating consumption

Reimer (1995) argues that young people's use of the mass media binds together their day (and hence their relationship with social change) more than any activity, for mass media consumption has a significant influence on both the public and the private sphere. Indeed, young people could even be said to be united through their pursuit of pleasure through the mass media. I have suggested throughout this book that the notion of young people's lifestyles, and in particular, consumer lifestyles, provide an invaluable means of coming to terms with what it means to be a young person at the turn of the millennium. The mass media constitute the primary vehicle for the transmission of global images of what these lifestyles 'should' consist, and hence play an influential role in legitimizing what is and what is not the appropriate lifestyle to adopt.

So here I am indeed suggesting that consumerism represents an important building-block upon which young people's lifestyles are built. But this statement is not necessarily an entirely negative one. Young people can use consumerism in positive ways, even if big business uses young people in the process. The relationship being described here is a *mutually* exploitative one. The Nintendo generation might themselves be described as a hedonistic generation. They use computer games for entertainment and to offset boredom. Pleasure is apparently what these young people are seeking. But by doing so they are creating a particular form of cultural expression in which they have control over how they fill their time. Global consumer capitalism may be overlooking this to some extent, but what bothers children and young people is how far their parents feel they are in control of their lives, and whether their peers are doing the same things that they are doing. It is in this sense that the Nintendo generation are entirely in control, and it is in this sense that the interactivity promoted by playing computer games is in itself liberatory.

The question remains, however, as to how far young people can control the media with which they interact and, perhaps most presciently, the extent to which consumer capitalism, actively directs that interaction. Although, like Rushkoff (1997), Côté and Allahar are most concerned with North American youth, their discussion of the power of the media in young people's lives is equally relevant in the British context in that they graphically illustrate the link between the media and the construction of lifestyles in a consumer society. Interestingly, Côté and Allahar (1996) discuss a piece of research conducted by Evans *et al.* (1991) in which they found that almost half of the total magazine space in young women's magazines was taken up by advertisements and that about half of these were concerned with selling beauty-care products, fashion, clothing and other products related to improving young people's appearances. The resources from which young people are interpreting their position in the world (however actively they may be doing so) are presenting them with a rather skewed idea of what that position should be – in this case, that position seems to promote young people as consumers of beautification. In other words, such magazines suggest to young people that in order to belong and in order to be fulfilled they need to partake in a consumer culture within which fashion trends and physical beautification are highly valued.

I am not suggesting for one minute that young people are entirely duped in the above scenario, but rather that they find themselves in a Catch-22 situation where basically they have very little choice but to construct consumer-based lifestyles. The magazines discussed by Evans *et al.* (which incidentally command an influential readership of around 2.5 million readers) promote a particular image of what it is to be a young woman, for example, and how happiness lies in beautifying yourself for the male gaze *via* consumption. The same concern is evident when you consider the influence of television, which more often than not portrays women as objects of youthful beauty as opposed to men who tend to be given more dominant and dynamic roles. But putting these specific points about gender to one side, the broader concern here is with the suggestion that young people are somehow being indoctrinated into an ethos based on 'consumerism, conformity, and immediate gratification' (Côté and Allahar 1996: 147). Côté and Allahar go on to argue that the way in which the mass media portray aspects of the outside world might be said to actively prevent young people from developing a critical consciousness that would allow them to prioritize larger issues of personal and social responsibility. Thus, as far as the magazines aimed at young people are concerned we need to ask whether these are simply reacting to a market need or whether, alternatively, they 'are specifically engineered to create a consciousness . . . which is then defined as a need' (Côté and Allahar 1996: 147). Côté and Allahar suggest that advertisers do indeed have an influential role to play in determining the content of magazines, largely because they want their particular products located close to articles on related issues (e.g. a hair spray close to an article on hair).

Both British and North American television seem to be overloaded with programmes aimed at consumers and often at young consumers. Côté and Allahar discuss an advertising flyer distributed in banks prior to the release of a Canadian television programme called 'Street Cents' which seems to suggest a programme aimed at helping young people to manage their finances, but which actually includes a cartoon incorporating the rallying call 'Buy it!' Côté and Allahar's somewhat controversial point of view is worth quoting at some length here:

> Since they are bombarded with tantalizing images of the 'good life', it is not surprising that the young are dispirited by the reality of their poor economic prospects . . . What lies at the heart of all this activity, however, is the fact that these media can sell young people some element of an identity they have been taught to crave . . . leisure industries such as music, fashion, and cosmetics have a largely uncritical army of consumers awaiting the next craze or fad. Each fad gives them a sense of identity, however illusory or fleeting. This activity is tolerated or encouraged by larger economic interests because the army of willing consumers also serves as a massive reserve of cheap labour. Furthermore, distracting young people with these 'trivial identity pursuits' prevents them from protesting against their impoverished condition.
>
> (Côté and Allahar 1996: 148–50)

The problem here appears to be that young people, perhaps more than any other social group, are not only the direct beneficiaries of the advantages of modern information technologies but also the victims of the drawbacks – both of which are mediated by global capitalism. One approach that has attempted to prioritize young people's perspectives within these sorts of ideological parameters is that of Marie Gillespie (1995) who has studied the way in which young people relate to Coca-Cola advertisements. Coca-Cola, as Gillespie suggests, appears to be a symbol of consumer capitalism, being well and truly part of every young person's repertoire of media knowledge. In particular, Gillespie talks about the Coca-Cola slogan 'you can't beat the feeling' and the double entendres encapsulated in this term that young people pick up on in their everyday exchanges. But the most interesting point as far as this book is concerned is that the Coca-Cola commercials portray the world to young people in a very particular way. They present a very idealized and particularized lifestyle to which young people are expected to aspire. Coca-Cola's image of the world is a utopian one where people sing, dance, socialize, have fun, fall in love and easily gain friends, status and popularity. In other words, everything a teenager could ever want from life. By watching these commercials young people can get 'the feeling' that they belong in this mythical world. It is well worth considering an exchange, quoted by Mackay (1997: 55–6), recorded among some young Asian people who were interviewed by Gillespie in Southall, London, which illustrates this point directly through the meanings young people attach to the media.

Sameera: My favourite ads are the Coca-Cola ads, they're American ads, I prefer American ads, I don't know why but I could watch them over and over again without getting bored [. . .]. I like them cos I just love drinking Coca-Cola [. . .]. I enjoy listening to the music [. . .]. I think the characters are fantastic. Every time I see the ad I always feel tempted to go out and buy it, even when I go out shopping, I always buy Coke cos, well, I love the ad [. . .].

Sukhi: Yeah, they're really happy and active cos they mix pop songs with kids in America, you know, the sun's always shining and everyone is smiling and it gives the impression of being free. The music and song puts more energy into it and like each line of the song is backed up with dancing, sports and fun [. . .]. 'You just can't beat the feeling!'

Gillespie (1995) suggests that young people are attracted by this portrayal of an American teenage lifestyle and as such the feelings ascribed by young people are conflated with the advertisement and the product:

By placing the ad in an idealised world of teenagers, free from parental and other constraints, a utopian vision of a teenage lifestyle is represented. The plausibility of the idyllic lifestyle and utopian relationships depicted by the ad is not questioned.

(Mackay 1997: 56)

The Coca-Cola advertisements portray a world full of harmonious relationships, fun and frolics – above all, a world where teenagers are free to be themselves. All this may imply again that young people are acutely uncritical of the mass media and in particular of advertising; but such a suggestion would be misleading. For instance, Gillespie also discusses a company called 'Rubicon' who produce tropical soft drinks advertised via a commercial which is centred upon a domestic scene in an Asian household. The young people Gillespie interviewed about these ads were very critical of the campaign, arguing that the product itself was badly designed, while complaining that one particular advertisement featuring an Indian family did so in an insulting derogatory manner. As such, the young people interviewed appeared to be particularly concerned that certain adverts and British television in general reinforced negative stereotypes of Asian families. It is also interesting to note, as Gillespie points out, that young people are not entirely aware of the subtlety of advertising: the fact for example that Coca-Cola is aimed directly at young people, while the Rubicon is intended for the consumption of British Asian families and more specifically Asian mothers.

The point here is that the young people interviewed by Gillespie were critical of the adverts concerned, but only within their immediate sphere of social influence. That is, they were critical of the Rubicon advert because they felt it implicated them as British Asians. Living in Southall, a well-established Asian community, many of them felt cut off from mainstream British society and in effect felt alienated due to the perception of them by the wider population as 'foreigners'. Thus when this stereotype is reproduced in the media they draw upon their everyday experience, which leads them to the conclusion that this commercial is offensive. On the other hand, the Coca-Cola advertisement works on the opposite principle in the sense that it appears to be promoting harmony between races and yet paradoxically and simultaneously the joys of a Western way of life. The Coca-Cola advert offers young Asians what Gillespie (1995) describes as 'an alternative space of fantasy identification' (p. 59). What I am suggesting here then is that young people are indeed critical of the media, but only as far as their immediate experience allows them to be. This therefore means they are potentially vulnerable, if vulnerable is indeed the right word, to forms of the mass media that propagate more subtle ideological messages. Young people are not dupes, but just like anybody else they interpret the mass media according to the actualities of their own everyday experience. In many respects that experience is bounded by the fact that young people live in a consumer society. The media do have a vested interest in creating and maintaining a certain consciousness among the young, as either a concession to their own economic interests through advertising or perhaps more directly through TV channels such as MTV, which is entirely devoted to promoting popular music. In effect, as Côté and Allahar (1996) suggest, the media is selling young people an element of an identity they have been taught to crave.

Discussion

The argument developed here is that the selling of consumer lifestyles via the mass media reflects broader aspects of social change, particularly the move towards individualization (discussed in Chapter 4). Young people have always been concerned with 'creating themselves' (see Boëthius 1995) but the actual aesthetic needs of young people appear to be stronger than ever before. The nature of media consumption has changed to the extent that we no longer need all-absorbing aesthetic experiences. Some commentators have argued that this has resulted in a dilution of quality to the extent that young people are no longer capable even of consuming intelligent ideas through the media, but are simply more suited to the superficial and punchy imagery of post-modern television (see Griffin 1993). From this point of view, young people's consumption of the media has therefore become more diverse, though often less intense than it may have been in the past. Young people are arguably more independent than they ever have been and as such

> They have become 'the pioneers of consumer society' (Drotner 1991: 49). In addition, the mass media's constantly expanding flow of information increases young people's knowledge of life. Via the media they are presented with all aspects of life long before they have a chance to experience them first hand.
>
> (Boëthius 1995: 151)

The mass media therefore plays an important role in structuring young people's relationships with consumer culture, while such relationships are most often acted out on an individual basis through TV sets or hi-fi's in young people's rooms. Steele and Brown (1995) specifically consider the relationship between the bedroom as a young person's haven and media use. They argue that young people are essentially active in their use of the media and that media use among young people is essentially dialectical. Individuals shape and transform their encounters with the media in 'a continuous cycle of meaning making' (p. 553). In this respect, the media is an important cultural agent whose influences on audiences are both amplified and restrained by active consumers. Equally interesting is Steele and Brown's (1995) suggestion that young people's sense of who they are plays a central role in their use of the media, while actively affecting identity constructions in the process. Steele and Brown's comments on this conclusion apply more generally to discussions of media influence. They point out that the media's affect on young people is highly complex and notoriously difficult to research precisely because that influence is realized through everyday activities and routines. The media, in effect infuses everyday life. More specifically, media use infuses young people's lifestyles.

The gap between the wealth of possibilities that the mass media appears to offer and the actualities of an everyday life characterized by insecurity and uncertainty appears to be widening without there appearing to be many means of redressing this balance. To conclude, it might be suggested that young people are indeed critical consumers of the mass media. Their relationship with the mass media is highly complex and in some respects ideologically loaded. The proposition that young people actively engage with the mass media and to a degree forge it in their own image is a sound one, but is only ever partially realized. Ultimately, the parameters within which young people are able to do so, are set down for them by a mass media that is inevitably constructed first and foremost on the need to sell magazines, programmes and what is essentially a consumerist way of life. Young people are therefore liberated and constrained by the mass media at one and the same time – it provides them with a canvas, but the only oils they can use to paint that canvas are consumerist ones. Osgerby (1998) therefore argues that media representations of youth are increasingly determined by lifestyle as opposed to age-related issues. I want to go one step further than this and suggest that young people do not consume the media according to their membership of particular youth subcultures but according to the everyday negotiation of their lifestyles. Young people have been reconstructed as consumers first and foremost, and any creativity on their part will almost inevitably involve the adaptation of consumerist media messages. From a critical point of view young people could therefore be dismissed as little more than fun-loving hedonists. This is a point of view I will consider more closely in Chapter 6, which will focus, in particular, on young people's relationship with rave culture.

Recommended reading

Buckingham, David (ed.) (1993) *Reading Audiences: Young People and the Media*. Manchester: Manchester University Press.
    A wide-ranging collection of articles which consider the extent to which young people actively interpret media messages.
Gillespie, Marie (1995) *Television, Ethnicity and Cultural Change*. London: Routledge.
    Particularly useful on the way in which young people relate to consumer culture through the mass media.
Osgerby, Bill (1998) *Youth in Britain Since 1945*. Oxford: Blackwell.
    An absolutely fascinating account of the historical emergence of youth within which there is a particularly enlightening discussion of media representations of young people.
Rushkoff, Douglas (1997) *Children of Chaos: Surviving the End of the World as We Know It*. London: Flamingo.
    A highly readable, though somewhat journalistic, discussion of young people as 'screenagers' at the cutting edge of media consumption at the turn of the century.

6
RAVING HEDONISTS?

Young people are hedonists. They are more concerned about enjoying themselves from one minute to the next than they are worried about what the future may or may not hold for them. If hedonism involves propping up the values of the dominant culture and of forfeiting their historical role, then so be it. The state of the environment, social inequality, access to Higher Education, all these issues pale into insignificance compared to the God-given right to party. Is this an accurate portrayal of what it is to be a young person at the beginning of the new millennium? Are young people really as apathetic and self-centred as this sort of an approach implies? What matters (and what doesn't matter) to young people at the end of the twentieth century, and how does an understanding of what matters to young people affect how we analyse the nature of youth lifestyles?

In order to provide a context in which the above issue can be discussed, I now want to consider in some depth the youth culture (if it can be described as such) most commonly described as representing youth lifestyles at the end of the twentieth century, namely that associated with dance or rave, while relating that discussion to wider concerns about the nature of social change and the construction of lifestyles. A preliminary understanding of how commentators view rave and the assumptions they make about rave as a reflection of the youth experience in general may well serve as a useful illustration of the way in which sociologies of youth fail to accurately comprehend what youth lifestyles are all about. In particular, I make the suggestion that super-ficial commentaries on rave and dance cultures have tended to valorize rave as somehow being representative of broader experiences of youth when in fact rave is arguably not representative of young people's every-day experience at all.

Alongside the somewhat misleading academic discussion of rave which I will discuss shortly, there has emerged a parallel and media-inspired moral panic emphasizing illegal aspects of dance culture through drug-induced scare stories. This has served to intensify a situation within which some key aspects of dance actually reinforce the very characteristics that the journalists and moral guardians of society claim is being undermined. In this chapter I suggest that young people have to some extent been subsumed within dominant power structures (most notably within the context of consumerism), of which rave represents one part. Young people are barely rebellious at all, least of all in the context of rave, but in fact are willing to go along with dominant ways of life if that means they can construct their own meanings around that way of life, if and when they see fit.

The emergence of rave

Rave culture first emerged in Britain in the late 1980s as *the* new youth cultural phenomena (see Smith and Maughan 1998). At first glance rave did indeed appear to challenge dominant power structures through illegal parties and drug use, and as a general affront to police author-ity. The arrival of Ecstasy in Britain saw what was essentially a musical phenomenon emerge as a cultural one (Redhead 1993; Smith and Maughan 1998) and in many respects, as Smith and Maughan suggest, the rave scene was quintessentially post-modern:

> The event, the rave, and the music were seen as the perfect post-modern experience; here was culture that couldn't be reproduced, it had to be experienced, even the artefacts used such as records were transformed through the DJ mixing them into something new, but something which only existed at that moment. Furthermore, it was also the place for the post-modern self; a rave has been seen as the site for the disappearance of the self, disappearance that embodied the 'pleasures of loss and abandonment'.
>
> (Smith and Maughan 1998: 218)

In his book *Energy Flash: A Journey Through Rave Music and Dance Culture*, Simon Reynolds (1998) goes as far as to suggest that Ecstasy has utterly transformed youth leisure in Britain and Europe. The fact that alcohol clouds the experience of Ecstasy has meant that aggression has been diminished, and the 'cattle market' atmosphere of so many clubs has been replaced by a far more conducive environment where young people of either sex are free to bond without the threat of unwanted sexual attention. In effect then, Reynolds (1998: 404) argues that Ecstasy and the rave culture that accompanies it promote tolerance in a country characterized by its stuffiness:

> One of the delights of the rave scene at its loved-up height was the way it allowed for mingling across class, race and sex-preference lines. MDMA rid club culture of its clique-ishness and stylish sectarianism; hence sociologist Sheila Henderson's phrase 'luvdup and de-élited'. Rave's explosive impact in the UK, compared with its slower dissemination in America, may have something to do with the fact that Britain remains one of the most rigidly class-stratified countries in the Western world.

In this context, Reynolds describes the controlled hedonism of the MDMA experience, pointing out as he does so that such an experience is in fact highly compatible with a conformist lifestyle. Manning (1996) also suggests that taking Ecstasy itself hardly constitutes a radical act, subverting little more than a person's sleep patterns. Ecstasy can be seen from this point of view to be as boring then, as the culture it symbolizes.

The above is an interesting point that would tend to corroborate a lot of the arguments that are being presented throughout this book, and most pointedly the suggestion that young people are not characterized by the sort of outrageous hedonistic behaviour often portrayed by the media. Rather, they behave in ways that barely threaten the dominant order, and which in many respects actually serve to bolster or re-energize that order. Thus, Reynolds describes the rave as a holiday from the mundanity of everyday life and an escape from the everyday 'you'. Both the mental and financial investment that a lot of young people put into a rave are tantamount to that of a short vacation and therefore could be suggested to represent little more than an escape from capitalist work patterns where batteries can be recharged and where ravers can experience a more fulfilling, if short-lived way of life. Reynolds (1998) discusses the work of Antonio Melechi (1993) who suggests that rather than deploying the exhibitionist rebellion of the subcultures of the 1960s and 1970s, rave represents a form of collective disappearance, amounting to more than simple disengagement in so far as it represents a form of unified collective disappearance (Reynolds 1998: 404). Melechi

(1993) describes the spectacular club scenes in resorts such as Rimini in Ibiza as 'pure consumerism' (p. 36) which in turn reflects the 'death of youth culture.' In this extract Melechi presciently sums up what rave culture represents from this point of view:

> This was a 'bleak generation' lost in a world of bacchanalian pleasures. The old language of resistance, empowerment and identity, which had claimed a long line of folk devils as the return of the repressed, was redundant in the face of a subculture whose rank and file were socially diverse. The more general problems for critics who would attempt to read youth and club culture, was the emergence of a scene without stars and spectacle, gaze and identification. Those who sought to understand this subculture in terms of a politics of usage and identity completely missed the point, the places which club culture occupied and transformed through Ecstasy and travel represent a fantasy of liberation, an escape from identity. A place where nobody is, but everybody belongs.
>
> (Melechi 1993: 37)

As Redhead (1993) points out in the same volume, one thing is sure: traditional subcultural modes of theorizing about youth cultures have been rendered obsolete in the context of rave culture which has in itself undermined traditional ideas about the role of youth culture.

Rave as mass culture?

How then should we go about analysing or interpreting the rave phenomenon? One approach might be to write it off as the straightforward product of a mass culture which is simply reproducing young people as dupes of a dehumanizing mass society. Indeed, if you start by considering the music underlying the rave phenomenon, dance cultures can easily be misinterpreted as epitomizing mass culture at its worst, as Thornton (1997) points out. The apparently standardized nature of the beats incorporated in dance music make it an easy target for critics of those so-called mindless forms of mass entertainment so vehemently dismissed by critical theorists such as Theodor Adorno (1990).

Adorno was a key member of the Frankfurt School of Critical Theory whose members were linked together by a concern with human freedom and the ways in which such freedom had been curtailed through forms of domination and suppression in the modern world. Central to the Frankfurt School's thesis was the argument that at the time they were writing in the 1920s and 1930s a growing void was emerging between elite centres of power and a disorganized culturally based mass which was inherently vulnerable to manipulation through the vulgarities of the mass media. The core of the Frankfurt School's position (as far as it is accurate to describe a single position) was that modern capitalism had in fact encouraged the development of a mass society in which the proletariat or the masses were highly atomized and unorganized, and as such easily swayed by irrational ideologies such as fascism. Theodor Adorno (in conjunction with Max Horkheimer) was more specifically concerned with the emergence of what they called the 'culture industries'. Horkheimer and Adorno (1973) saw capitalist culture as being essentially false, amounting to little more than a pre-packaging of flat ideas. From this point of view music was becoming increasingly pacifying and repressive, promoting conformity while impeding critical judgement. Horkheimer and Adorno therefore saw modern culture as producing safe, standardized products geared to the larger demands of a capitalist economy:

> The culture industry perpetually cheats its consumers of what it perpetually promises. The promissory note which, with its plots and staging, it draws on pleasure is endlessly prolonged; the promise, which is actually all the spectacle consists of, is illusory: all it actually confirms is that the real point will never be reached, that the diner must be satisfied with the menu.
>
> (Horkheimer and Adorno 1973: 139)

As far as Horkheimer and Adorno were concerned then, music simply regurgitates the same ideas over and over again through a process of 'pseudo-individualization'. The essential structure of popular music remains the same, though with very slight changes in detail, and so appeals to the lowest common denominator of mass consumer taste while conveniently satisfying the consumer's need for a sense of individuality, however false that sense might be. In essence then, music, and in particular popular music, becomes little more than a vehicle for the standardization of audience reaction alongside the maximization of economic dividends. The young consumer of popular forms of music is therefore hoodwinked by its familiarity which flatters him or her into reproducing the dominant social norms of a capitalistic society. Adorno and Horkheimer's work has been the subject of considerable criticism, not least that of intellectual snobbery and cultural elitism. However, it is also fair to say that the approach evident in the Frankfurt School's work, if not their conclusions, is highly insightful in so far as it raises important issues about the ideological role of popular cultural forms. It could therefore be argued that rave and the musical forms that underpin it, notably through the prominence of the DJ and the remix, are entirely uncreative and simply provide a mass cultural mode of escape that props up the capitalist system. At least at one level, then, Adorno and Horkheimer's work in some ways closely relates to aspects of dance, which is so dependent on regular (and arguably monotonous) beats. However, in other respects, their approach is too simplistic to be entirely appropriate for an analysis of dance culture.

Above all, this sort of an approach underestimates the meanings people invest in the *culture* that surrounds dance music. For as Thornton (1997) argues, club cultures are above all taste cultures which house fluid conceptions of what constitutes authentic and legitimate expressions of popular culture. Ecstasy, in turn, isn't just a substance to be consumed or banned, but is actually a cultural phenomenon in itself (Manning 1996). Dance music is a live phenomenon, characterized by the escapist liberatory atmosphere of the club. Many authors, including Manning (1996), have gone as far as to describe Ecstasy as the classic product of the nihilistic 80s, reflecting the desire to live for the moment and the need to prioritize style over content. As Manning (1996: 41) states, 'it's as true of acid as Ecstasy that the main incentive for indulging was and is getting blitzed out of your brain'. In this sense, it could well be argued that rave does in fact express aspects of young people's relationship to a dominant mass culture, and although the power of that culture to control young people should not be exaggerated, it should at least be acknowledged. To this end I will now discuss rave as an aspect of mass consumption.

Rave as mass consumption?

It is certainly true to say that the evolution of rave has been characterized by a move towards commercialization. Despite the superficial impression of rave as rebellion or opposition, at its core lies the reproduction of commercially driven values associated with that dominant order. And as rave evolved, as Smith and Maughan (1998) point out, it was this aspect that came to dominate. The commercial rave scene emerged as a far more enduring proposition than its underground counterpart. The 1994 Public Order Act introduced specific anti-rave legislation and thereby played some role in ensuring that rave became a more organized, commercialized and urbanized scene. At one and the same time, however, the commercialized rave scene came to be characterized by depthlessness and hyper-reality (Reynolds 1998: 23). Such hyper-reality is represented by a plethora of rave 'scenes' from 'handbag house' to 'ambient' and 'happy hardcore'. But as Reynolds (1998) points out, all this could be said to add up to little more than the ultimate expression of post-modernism, 'culture without content, without an external referent' (p. 106). Rave is energetic and appears to ooze meaning, but in the end that meaning is futile in that it simply serves to 'line the pockets of the promoter, and Mr. Evian' (p. 106). In this sense rave culture is a culture of contradictions, providing a fantastic sense of fulfilment alongside a hollow sense of emptiness:

> With E, the full-on raver means literally falling in love every weekend, then (with the inevitable mid-week crash) having your heart broken. Millions of kids across Europe are still riding this emotional roller-coaster. Always looking ahead to their next tryst with E, dying to gush, addicted to love, in love with . . . nothing . . . If you're right in the thick of it, the minutiae of the music's evolution, the endless search for the perfect breakbeat, the to-and-fro dialogue of jungle's collective creativity, well it's totally enthralling. Step outside its parameters for a moment, though, and you might think jungle, or any post-rave scene, is more a case of 'get a life' than 'way of life': a pseudo-culture, in other words.
>
> (Reynolds 1998: 107)

The implicit suggestion here is that rave does not necessarily have any deep meaning beyond what we can identify on the surface. But if young people are hedonists why should we object? Why should young people be assumed to be in opposition to any particular dominant order? Why shouldn't they simply consume for consumption's sake? Well perhaps the concern in this context lies in the fact that as a cultural phenomenon rave arguably became dominated by producers rather than consumers. The move towards a commercial form of dance culture came to say more about the values of society in general than it did about the values of young people. Jayne Miller (1995) brings together the sentiments of the 'New Generation X' in her collection *Vox Pop* in which she attempts to give young people a voice. As an editor of a Leeds-based fanzine, *The Herb Garden*, David Gill's comments in Miller's book are especially pertinent here:

> Dance has become a massive popular culture. Now it's all about money-making, merchandising and selling T-shirts. The raves as they were have gone . . . The problem is if people can't stop it, they commercialise it. Cash in on it and popularise the culture. It happened with punk, it will always happen.
>
> (Miller 1995: 111)

Birgit Richard and Heinz Hermann Kruger (1998) consider this issue in the context of the German techno scene. They argue that rave amounts to a suspension of everyday rules and that any potential for political message can only be expressed through patterns of love and friendship, as opposed to political action of any real sort. Despite the existence of an underground scene, at its heart techno is a very commercialized form of youth culture and can be associated with particular forms of clothing (e.g. club wear, Technokit), food (e.g. energy drinks) and even commercialized sports such as snowboarding (Richard and Kruger 1998: 171). Far from maintaining a critical voice from without of the dominant culture, ravers could well be said to be subsumed from within.

Rave as hedonistic individualism?

The commercialization and formalization of rave has apparently ensured that it has become less a way of life and more a way of weekend-life where party-going hedonism is the be all and end all. But in order to understand the implications of rave culture for young people's lifestyles in general, it is very important to avoid the temptation to take the legacy of traditional youth approaches too literally, as Gelder and Thornton (1997) point out. The development of the Birmingham School and the principles that underlie it ensured that portrayals of young people have been over-politicized (see Chapter 1). In other words, there might be a tendency to dismiss rave as being of no actual interest to the sociologist of youth precisely because it tells us very little about the political motivations of young people. What it does tell us about is their *lack* of political motivation which is of at least equal concern in that this sea change reflects the changing nature of youth lifestyles.

It is absolutely crucial therefore that youth cultures are not conceptualized independently of the social conditions within which they operate. As far as the emergence of youth or club cultures at the end of the twentieth century is concerned, it is important to discuss the broader emergence of what some authors have described as 'hedonistic individualism' which characterized British society from the late 1980s through the early 1990s and which in turn had important implications for the changing nature of youth culture during this period and beyond (see Marquand and Seldon 1996; Barker 1997; Redhead 1997).

Hedonistic individualism apparently replaced the moralistic individualism of the late 1970s and early 1980s that had prioritized Victorian values alongside a guilt culture built upon the foundations of expanding market forces. The political problem at hand here, as Marquand (1996) points out, is that the Conservative party's moral vision was at odds with its economic vision which eventually emerged all-dominant, in the form of a period characterized by easy credit, tax cutting and a consumer boom. The vigorous virtues of moral individualism had, in effect, given way to the easy-going vices of an increasingly hedonistic culture (Marquand 1996). Thatcherism did not create the desires associated with conservative individualism, but responded to them and subsequently appropriated them (Leadbetter 1989). As Leadbetter goes on to point out, Thatcherism built up its vision of how society should be organized from a 'narrow account of the acquisitive, defensive drives which motivate individuals as consumers' (p. 137). But as far as Leadbetter is concerned, this version of individualism constitutes more than straightforward hedonism in the sense that the social philosophy it reflects is far broader through 'the possibility of individuals becoming agents to change their worlds through private initiatives' (p. 142).

Hedonism implies the straightforward seeking of pleasure. But the individualism that the Conservatives propagated in the 1980s depended on an ideology based on the principles of rationality, discipline, responsibility and power. People, and not least young people, were therefore convinced that they had the power to remake their own worlds. Unfortunately, that power was only able to take them so far. For young people in particular, the consumerist promise could never be fulfilled because somebody had to pay for the freedom of the market and young people were first in line for the firing squad. Despite this, young people were at least able to construct dance cultures as private initiatives. Rave was and is hedonistic in that, through it, young people have prioritized the right to party. However, perhaps what is more fundamental in a more general discussion of youth lifestyles is the fact that the public face of youth culture became less important to young people who were not concerned with sticking two fingers up to society (although the media became insistent that they were), but rather preferred to construct their own private world within which they could construct their own private meanings. Ironically, even this apparently minor request was denied by a Conservative government evidently over-zealous in its desire to keep rave in its place through the Entertainments (Acid House) Increased Penalty Act of 1990 and the Criminal Justice and Public Order Act of 1994.

What then do changes on the political landscape mean for the changing nature of society in general? Kingdom (1992: 1) goes as far as to describe the emergence of a 'masturbatory society' where fulfilment becomes a solitary pastime, free of the complications arising from moral demands by others. This cultural climate emerged on the back of a political one based on what Kingdom (1992: 2) describes as 'an unstable amalgam of economic liberalism, monetarism, anti-corporatism, authoritarianism and populism'. Thus, the New Right gave a momentum to free-market principles, not only through the market, but also in the wider social and, in turn, the cultural arena. Rave is arguably therefore simply a reflection of these broader changes, changes based on the justification that

> Psychologically it is argued that it is natural, that each person is governed by an unquenchable instinct for self-preservation, a desire to look out for the self, to pull up the ladder and 'never do owt for nowt, unless thee does it for thissen'. Any social system that does not take this hard fact into account will be naively utopian and doomed to failure. The utilitarian argument goes further, insisting that if each person acts according to naked self-interest, the end result will be the best for society. Life is a great game of cricket, where if each player scores as many runs as possible, the team will triumph.
>
> (Kingdom 1992: 6)

Kingdom therefore charts the emergence of an ideology which directly opposes the collectivist notion of a society that is based upon fulfilling the common good. As such, individualism is founded on selfishness, love for oneself rather than one's neighbours. By constructing their own escapist world of mutual abandonment young people reject this ideology on the surface and yet simultaneously reinforce it. They promote an environment in which people use Ecstasy in order that people do love each other, but they do so not with any intention of changing the masturbatory society Kingdom describes, but rather simply to provide a short-lived release valve from it, before they return to it refreshed the next day.

This theme is extended by Andrew Calcutt (1998) in his book *Arrested Development*. Here he argues that counter-cultures are in fact *victim* cultures which, far from being liberatory, actively play a role in negating human potential. In this context, Calcutt discusses the significance of Ecstasy which serves to provide the user with warmth, security and a general sense of well-being. For Calcutt, the role of Ecstasy is as an antidote to a prevailing atmosphere of risk and anxiety. Despite media-hype about the risks inherent in taking Ecstasy, Calcutt is insistent that its main role is the opposite to that suggested by its critics:

far from threatening the lives of those young people who take it, Ecstasy releases those who consume it from the perceived threat of victimization. This development is seen to reflect a low point in the history of human endeavour. In the 'nervous nineties', the arena of youth culture was more about banal empathy than rebellious risk-taking. In this sense Calcutt argues that the E-scene is more immature than any previous incarnations of youth culture because it is self-consciously *un*rebellious. Youth lifestyles therefore appear to be changing primarily because individualization has come to have such a profound impact on the nature of social life. Meanwhile, there is undoubtedly a very thin line between individualization and individualism.

Young people, rave and the market

If we therefore return to the question of rave and dance as hedonism, one interpretation might be that the instabilities faced by young people have come to play a more fundamental role in their lives than the fantasies of a better life that dominated in the 1980s. During the 1990s, therefore, young people became increasingly discontented and demotivated, and consequently started to live purely for the present, their faith in the future having been entirely eroded. As far as happiness is possible in this context, the immediacy of the consumer culture became a solution, albeit a transient solution to their problems. As Keane (1997) argues, 'leisure became [young people's] religion and, for a time, their saviour . . . The general public were unhappy despite the apparent good state of the economy, because their well being had been the price for its success' (p. 128).

From this point of view Ecstasy is the symbol of what is essentially an unhappy society, the problem being that Thatcher's and Major's children's identities were born in the epistemological free-for-all of the 1980s and 1990s which, in turn, produced a generation of street-wise intelligent realists. As far as Keane is concerned, what is unique about youth culture nowadays is nothing more than the free market that underlies it:

> Youth live in a hyper-real world where they can buy and sustain the look they want, the music they want, even the type of friends they want, by organising into a visible market segment. Those who cannot afford to do so respond with the same consumerist spirit and create their own complex street cultures and black markets.
>
> (p. 132)

In contemporary youth cultures free market ideals can therefore be said to permeate every aspect of life, and the end-product of such ideals is a period of youth that is in many ways more grown up than an adulthood 'that still adheres to a corporatist logic of work and social responsibility' (Keane 1997: 131). Young people are not attracted by the economic certainties of such an existence, but apparently opt for the alluring world of the hyper-real instead. Young people then exist in what Keane (1997: 132) describes as a cultural tornado:

> Psychologically, youth are displaced and disoriented, relentlessly thrown up into the air by the promise of consumer fulfilment. A quick fix with an empty culture leaves them dazed and confused and flying back for more. Yet, like the Wizard of Oz, behind its impressive surface, this culture has no real stability or power to confer. Not even DKNY ruby slippers can magic the young to somewhere that feels like home'.

Rave therefore represents a misguided effort on the part of young people to take control. They cannot take control of anything else, so they take control of their bodies. This provides a welcome relief from the 'empty chatter of the market culture', but ultimately it simply refuels young people's desire to be part of a culture they question, on the one hand, but would not want to be without on the other. Rave is, in effect, as empty as the culture it attempts (or rather does not attempt) to critique. Many commentators have indeed labelled rave as the 'last subculture' in that it represents a unique combination of alternative lifestyles alongside a relentless reproduction of commercialism (see Huq 1997).

There appears to be substantial evidence to suggest that consumerism plays a key role in structuring aspects of young people's lifestyles. As such, the hedonists' life is organized around the playing out of fantasies and daydreams through the pursuit of sensual pleasure, and such pleasures appear to be available through consumption. In this sense, it might be argued that consumerism, hedonism and individualism have undermined traditional ways of living, and that one of those ways of living is the traditional youth subculture. Indeed, 'when everything can be bought and sold, all human relations reduced to those of producer and consumer of commodities, then other forms of sovereignty become difficult to maintain' (Abercrombie 1994: 45).

Interestingly, Osgerby (1998) goes on to discuss the extent to which the prominence of the dance and rave scenes in British youth culture presents a collapse of boundaries between subcultural 'authenticity' and commercial 'fabrication'. He argues that subcultural originality has become increasingly hard to distinguish from straightforward commercial exploitation. The implication that there was previously a clear divide between genuine subcultural forms and those expressed either commercially or through the media is at best a misleading one. Osgerby argues that the market and in particular the process of exchange has always played an important role in shaping youth cultural forms, while the media has always played a pivotal role in transmitting coherent subcultural formations. The commercial market has indeed always played an influential part in the construction of youth culture and subcultures. This much can be accepted. But on the other hand, the thesis underlying this book is that these commercial influences are closer to the surface of contemporary youth culture than they ever have been before and this reflects a process whereby young people are far more adept (and yet ironically vulnerable) consumers than they ever have been before. In a world where the image of the so-called sovereign consumer is increasingly prevalent, the reality is such that the market has more and more control over what constitute young people's lifestyles, precisely because the rhetoric that goes along with market forces creates the illusion that young people are freer to control those lifestyles. But what is actually going on is an intensification of processes of global conformity.

In some respects youth culture is also heterogeneous, notably in terms of the number of different varieties of dance available to young people. In this context, authors such as Osgerby (1998) and Bhaba (1990) have identified a state of 'translation', a widening of potential race identities based on a cross-fertilization of cultural traditions. In some respects then, the resigned pessimistic analyses of a depthless and media-saturated post-modern culture, as outlined in the work of authors such as Baudrillard (1983) and Jameson (1984), has to be tempered by an acknowledgement of the potentially liberating dislocation of identity positions that are actually entailed (Osgerby 1998: 204). Young people can indeed be said to be at the centre of a process of de-centring where the stability of modern identities appear to have been superseded by the fragmented and hybrid nature of youth cultures such as dance. But perhaps the abiding characteristic of youth lifestyles at the end of the twentieth century is uncertainty, a suggestion which in itself undermines any notion of youthful hedonism. Such hedonism may serve young people and their right to party, but ultimately it is more influential in propping up dominant ideologies. I have often suggested that in some ways young people can usefully be described as barometers of social change, but perhaps in this context they are equally important as indicators of social continuity. Young people have traditionally had to deal with the stresses and strains of economic and social change. In a

consumer-dominated world, the images of 'youth-as-fun' that dominated the middle years of the century appear to have been dissipated to
the extent that

> by the early nineties any concept of the teenager as the embodiment
> of hedonistic consumption had become untenable. The commercial
> market that had provided the motor for the post-war 'teenage
> revolution' had been undercut by a combination of the demo-
> graphic contraction of the youth population, growing levels of
> youth unemployment and a widening gap between youth and adult
> rates of pay.
>
> (Osgerby 1998: 208)

In developing this point, Osgerby discusses the emergence of 'grunge'
among teenagers in the late 1980s. Based on angstful expressions of dis-
illusionment, characterized most clearly in the music of Nirvana whose
lead singer, Kurt Cobain, committed the classic rock suicide, grunge
apparently represented a rejection of dominant aspirational values and
a general indifference to the world in general. Grungers were unkempt,
untidy, uninterested and unqualified and as such were forced to retreat
into 'a listless life of casual jobs and capricious leisure' (Osgerby 1998:
209). According to Osgerby then, the abiding characteristic of grungers
as a metaphor for youth in general was that of bleak, meaningless lives
and pessimistic attitudes reflecting upon a world that had apparently
left young people behind.

But grungers are not wholly representative of youth lifestyles at the
end of the twentieth century. Indeed, many of the stylistic aspects of
grunge is evident in the lifestyles of surfers who have established their
own particular youth culture, most notably along the south coast of
Britain. Surfers, like young people in general, do not have vast amounts
of money, but this does not necessarily prevent them from maximizing
their resources in order that they can have the best possible time. Young
male surfers often dye their hair blond to reflect, perhaps, their fun-
loving philosophy. The need to surf and to be seen to surf appears to
be a way of life for many young people intent on living life on the edge.
A whole youth style has emerged around this principle – there are now
even urban surfers who speed around town centres in south-west Britain
on their oversize skateboards, apparently anxious to maintain the sort
of lifestyle many of us would more readily associate with people in their
early teens. A distinct surf-fashion has also emerged, not only in the
form of clapped out VW vans which can transport the surfer, his mate,
and their equipment, but also in terms of surfing fashions and brands

that reflect the commercial undercurrent to the subculture in general. If they indeed exist at all, subcultures legitimize a world in which opposition is dead and consumer lifestyles are alive and well.

Given this, there could be an argument for suggesting that youth subcultures are precisely one of those forms of sovereignty that appears to have been undermined by the emergence of market-led hedonistic principles. Youth culture has always been closely related to consumer culture or at least to a denial of that culture. But at the end of the twentieth century youth culture is powerless to deny the forward thrust of consumerism as a way of life because the more young people pursue the escape that rave and dance offers them the more they will reinforce the consumerist ideal. As Malbon (1998) suggests, the point about dance cultures is not that they represent a struggle with a dominant, hegemonic culture, but that they provide an everyday arena of

> resistance on a micro-level, on the level of everyday life, where the unspoken is that which binds the group together, where the desire to be with others is manifested, and differences are addressed. This is resistance as found in the dynamic and exciting combination of musics, in the fleeting pause before the DJ drops the bass in, in the semi-visibility of a darkened dance floor, in taking Ecstasy (in not taking Ecstasy), in dressing in a certain way, in the emotional and empathetic effects of close proximity to hundreds of others, not necessarily like yourself, but sharing, at the very least, a desire to be right there, right now. This is the resistance found through losing your self, paradoxically to find yourself.
>
> (Malbon 1998: 280–1)

Rave is potentially subversive, but can ultimately only be subversive in a submissive form.

Discussion

What does all this mean in the context of a discussion of post-modern hedonism? As we enter the twenty-first century are young people using hedonistic lifestyles in authentic productive ways in order to construct some semblance of identity in what is essentially an unstable world? At the very least, as I discussed in Chapter 4, rapid developments in communications technology, notably in the form of satellite and cable TV and increased power of multinational corporations, can certainly be said to have intensified processes of globalization, and groups of young people far removed from one another in terms of time and space became audiences for the same sets of messages and images and, in many respects, came to share the same cultural vocabulary. By the early nineties, therefore, it was possible for the first time to speak of a 'global' dimension to many youth styles and cultures.

(Osgerby 1998: 199–200)

As I argued in Chapter 5, the youth experience appears to have been de-territorialized. Young people are less dependent on the immediate expression of style in local contexts, because such styles are constantly reaffirmed anyway through the power of the global media and through the power of global processes of individualization.

The point I am trying to make here is that the hedonistic lifestyles, which have always characterized young people's lives to some extent since the 1950s, have had to be tempered in recent years due to the increasingly insecure nature of the youth experience. But young people still behave in hedonistic ways within the limited parameters provided for them by dominant social structures. One author who has attempted to come to terms with this issue is the cultural anthropologist Ted Polhemus (1994) who argues that popular culture, and with it youth culture, has become a defining feature of what constitutes centre stage. According to Polhemus, the influence of the media is such that young people are far more knowing than previous generations and this in itself has helped to create a generation of nostalgics and retro-freaks (see Chapter 5). Young people therefore pick and choose their youth culture, like they would cans of soup from a supermarket. Young people are, from this point of view, stylistically promiscuous. On the surface, the ideologies behind the youth cultures that young people adopt are not as important to them as in the past, but in fact they are buying into a complete semiological package within which they are more than aware of the appropriate meanings relevant to each style, but simply do not see the need to shout about these meanings in a way that would undermine their authenticity.

The above argument can be related to my earlier discussion of the fragmentation of rave which reflects the emergence of what Polhemus (1994) calls a quick-change 'Style World', 'where no one "uniform" would become a straightjacket' (p. 132). The supermarket of style therefore represents a significant change in the role and experience of youth cultures. It amounts to a sort of experimental laboratory which rejects the idea that young people can exchange a sense of belonging for a life-long stylistic and ideological commitment. However, the implication that this means that young people are simply hedonists out to have a good time is also misleading. As Polhemus suggests, 'underneath all the fancy dress and the posturing there is an attempt to construct a new visual language which will make it possible to say something fresh in an age when we've heard it all before' (p. 134). Contemporary youth cultures are therefore seen to be about mixing and matching, about the juxtaposition of styles and above all the playing with meanings. Young people are not simply slates upon which styles can be drawn, but are actively aware of and engage with the subcultural meanings which they are mixing.

> Streetstyle is not what it used to be – we are all too sophisticated to relive those days when standing around on a streetcorner in a leather jacket was a simple, exuberant act of rebellion – but it is still a remarkably illuminating reflection of the time and a succinct, powerful and alluring vision of the alternative.
>
> (Polhemus 1994: 134)

Regardless of the pseudo-freedom young people can establish in the supermarket of style, and regardless of the escape that rave and dance provides them with, hedonism, and more specifically hedonistic individualism, has won through to some extent as the totem of youth cultures at the end of the twentieth century. Regardless of how many people are disenfranchized from the consumer society, they are encouraged to believe that they can be fulfilled through what they buy and how they construct their own very 'individualistic' lifestyles. It is in this respect that a consumerist ideology has apparently become the dominant influence on youth lifestyles in contemporary Britain.

A fundamental problem with the sociology of youth, as I noted in Chapter 1, is that it has tended to privilege melodramatic expressions of youth at the expense of young people in general. This is ironic when the actual underpinnings of young people's relationship to the social world is more fruitfully understood in the context of routine everyday expressions of what it is to be a young person. To this end, Bob Hollands' (1995) study of young people's nightlife in Newcastle provides a useful end-point. The core of his argument is that the actual process of 'going out' has been transformed in recent years from a simple 'rite of passage' to a permanent 'socialising ritual' (p. 1); a process which itself reflects broader changes in economic, domestic and cultural life. Hollands argues that 'going out', and in particular the ritualistic tour of the Bigg Market area of Newcastle, provides a space in which young people actively construct their identities. This reflects the fact that consumption has emerged as a more central element in the production of youth identities. Involvement in what may appear on the surface to be little more than hedonistic self-indulgent alcohol consumption can therefore be argued to reflect and stand in for the loss of traditional identities. In effect, 'going out' represents the equivalent of 'community' to these young people, and as such is arguably not hedonistic at all, but rather reflects a deep-seated need to belong in an ever-changing world. What is interesting is that consumption provides the canvas upon which the need to belong is acted out. Hollands found that young people were willing to undergo debt and family conflict in order to retain the group solidarity that 'going out' provided them with. Certainly, the culture that Hollands describes does fulfil a need for excitement in what for many young people is an essentially mundane world, but it also provides a positive arena for mutual companionship. In this sense the superficial impression of hedonism does not necessarily tell the whole story. This, indeed, reflects a wider problem characteristic of the sociology of youth in general, namely the tendency for commentators to dwell on the immediate expression of youth, without an adequate attempt to comprehend both the immediate and the more long-term factors underlying such expressions.

This chapter has begun to consider the suggestion that young people's relationship to dominant power structures and the ways in which they often reproduce those structures is a constituent part of youth lifestyles at the end of the twentieth century. Young people's experience of social change is essentially paradoxical. The risks and instabilities of young people's lives appear to be stabilized and yet destabilized at one and the same time, partly at least because such instability is an essential prerequisite for the continued prosperity of consumer capitalism. This is the sort of issue I will be considering in more detail in the next chapter when I focus more closely on young people as consumers.

Recommended reading

Calcutt, Andrew (1998) *Arrested Development: Popular Culture and the Erosion of Adulthood*. London: Cassell.
  A good overall discussion of the changing dimensions of youth. The discussion of Ecstasy as an antidote to risk is particularly interesting.
Hollands, Robert (1995) *Friday Night, Saturday Night*. Newcastle: Newcastle University Press.
  Provides an empirical examination of young people's night-time leisure which manages to bring the study of cultural aspects of youth back down to earth.

Redhead, Steve (ed.) (1993) *Rave Off: Politics and Deviance in Contemporary Youth Culture*. Aldershot: Avebury.
A classic, if somewhat patchy, discussion of rave and how ravers interact with rave.
Reynolds, Simon (1998) *Energy Flash: A Journey Through Rave Music and Dance Culture*. London: Picador.
A fascinating and eye-opening account of dance culture and the role of music within that culture.

7
CONSUMING YOUTH

If young people are valued as anything in contemporary society that value lies in their role as consumers (Palladino 1996). As Griffin (1997) suggests, the actual significance of youth as an age-stage in many ways appears to lie in the fact that it is represented as the point at which human beings enter the production/reproduction/consumption cycle as adults. In this context, Wyn and Whyte (1997) go as far as to argue that 'today youth itself is a consumable item, in that the superficial trappings of youth are now part of the consumer market' (pp. 86–7). But can young people's experience of consumption really be adequately described as 'superficial'? Why is consumption so important to young people and what role does it play in constructing their relationship with society? Starkey (1989) argues that modern society's initiation rites have an oddly consumerist ring about them. Young people grow up by riding a bicycle, drinking beer, smoking or buying a stereo, a car or a house. These are the rites of passage we associate with a consumer society. Young people are, in effect, socialized into treating money and consumption as the doorway to life. In this chapter I intend to chart the emergence of young people as consumers before considering more specifically the role consumption plays as an arena in which young people construct their lifestyles at the end of the twentieth century. This should provide a framework within which more empirical material can be discussed in Chapter 8.

The development of the youth market

Any attempt to answer the questions posed above should begin with a discussion of the historical emergence of young people as consumers. Much like protracted discussions over the emergence of a consumer revolution, there is considerable debate as to when young people emerged as a market in their own right. What is certain is that the youth market did not emerge overnight. There is some evidence to suggest that young people were beginning to sample the attractions of consumer culture prior to the Second World War, the aftermath of which is more often seen to be a turning point. Perhaps most interestingly, David Fowler (1995) charts the rise of the teenage consumer in inter-war Britain. He argues that young people experienced a higher standard of living than the rest of the family, even among working-class families experiencing poverty. Citing a series of studies into household budgets during the 1920s, Fowler argues that a distinctive youth market began to emerge in Britain by the 1930s, notably with the appearance of a range of magazines and film titles expressly aimed at young wage-earners. Meanwhile, the dance halls opening up in working-class areas of Britain during the 1930s provided further evidence that young people were spending their money beyond the confines of the family unit. Significantly, Fowler points out that young people were not merely passive recipients of commercialized leisure but also consumed actively in the privacy of their own homes by spending their earnings on hobbies, for example. Perhaps most revealing in this regard is Fowler's reference to a piece in the *Manchester Guardian* in October 1926:

> Grandmothers and bishops, preaching from their armchairs and pulpits, insist that this is the Age of Luxury . . . short skirts, lipsticks, vulgar films . . . sex novels, jazz, the Eton crop . . . There is almost no end to the list of abominations . . . Before the war and in the easy years which immediately followed it, luxury was mainly a matter of means. Now any young typist from Manchester or Kensington can keep her hair trimmed and waved and her busy feet in fine stockings and pale kid shoes.
>
> (Fowler 1993: 106)

Fowler identifies a distinctive teenage culture based on the access to commercialized leisure and the conspicuous consumption of leisure-based products and services in British towns and cities. By the 1930s, wage-earners in working-class families had become the main beneficiaries of these new lifestyles; lifestyles that leisure entrepreneurs were more than keen to exploit.

But such patterns were not purely leisure-based, as Palladino (1996) notes in his discussion of the development of a middle-class high school market of 'character-building' consumption in the United States. Such a market was promoted most graphically by *Seventeen* magazine which transmitted mixed messages of young people as serious fully-fledged citizens alongside advertising images of self-improving products. These products and the advertising associated with them were intended to attract middle-class teenagers apparently intent on following their parents' conservative domestic footsteps. In some respects, youth consumption in the 1940s appeared to be little more than a case of adulthood-in-training, and as such, young people were yet to actively construct or at least participate in their own markets.

Despite exhaustive efforts by some commentators to chart the expenditure of disposable incomes on leisure pursuits prior to 1945 (see, for example, Fowler 1995), there appears to be a consensus in the literature that the youth market really came into its own in the aftermath of the Second World War, by which time young people were more able to release the shackles of pseudo-adulthood. Perhaps the most convincing argument to this end, and one worth considering in some detail, is that presented by Osgerby (1998). Though acknowledging that subcultural groups had existed among young people since the nineteenth century and that the seeds of a commercial youth market began to flourish between the wars, Osgerby is insistent that the Second World War provided a major turning point in ensuring that youth emerged as an influential social group in its own right. More so than ever before, young people were establishing themselves as their own distinct cultural entity and were therefore emerging as an increasingly attractive prospect to the market. In particular, as Osgerby (1998) notes, improved economic prospects saw a growth in demand for unskilled and semi-skilled labour and young people therefore constituted an increased proportion of the workforce. In 1947 an Official Government Paper drew attention to the increasing influence and financial self-sufficiency of the young worker:

> when young juvenile workers are scarce, as they are now, and are likely to continue to be, he [*sic*] quickly realises that he may not be so unimportant as he seemed at first; and after two or three years his income may be larger compared with his needs and with his contribution to his maintenance than at any other periods of his life.
>
> (Ministry of Education 1947)

In the post-war years, as Osgerby points out, young people became increasingly associated with affluence, an association that was popularized by Abrams' (1959) work on the teenage consumer in which he identified a 100 per cent increase in discretionary spending among young people. Despite various problems that Osgerby (1998) has identified in Abrams' (1959) methodology, there is considerable evidence to suggest that young people's earnings did rise in the post-war era and that they were at least experiencing relative prosperity (Osgerby 1998: 26). What is perhaps most interesting about these broad trends is that they constituted a largely working-class phenomenon, as ironically this was the time when the middle classes were taking advantage of longer periods in secondary education and were therefore in some respects excluded from the opportunities consumption might have afforded them.

By the 1950s and 1960s the youth market was really coming to fruition, as Gaines (1991) suggests, and young people were thus able to exploit a situation where they had increasing spending power but none of the responsibilities of their parents:

> Rebels or not, baby-boom teenagers demonstrated an unprecedented ability to open their parents' wallets, and that made all the difference in the world of commerce. Whether they were screaming for the Beatles, protesting an unpopular war, or experimenting with a counterculture of sex, drugs, and rock 'n' roll, teenagers were now the center of commercial attention.
>
> (Palladino 1996: xviii)

Davis (1990) notes that by the 1950s average teenage earnings had increased by over 50 per cent in real terms in comparison with the pre-war years. It was during this period, as Stewart (1992) points out, that fashions, entertainments, foods and drinks came onto the market, specifically aimed at satisfying the 'needs' of the young consumer. Though young people's spending did not account for a large percentage of overall consumer spending at this time, the fact that their spending tended to be concentrated on non-essential sectors made them an especially attractive proposition to the market. Young people found themselves in a unique position: they benefited from the newly found affluence of their parents and yet had none of their financial burdens (Stewart 1992).

Within the boundaries provided by the culture industries young people were actively able to carve out their own autonomy, an autonomy that was expressed through distinctive purchasing styles and patterns of consumption (Furlong and Cartmel 1997). In effect, young people continued to take advantage of an economic situation in which manufacturers and service industries demanded their labour, as well as the money being earned by their parents. As MacInnes (1961) commented at the time:

> we are in the presence . . . of an entirely new phenomenon in human history: that youth is rich. Once, the 'jeunese dorée' were a minute minority; now, all the young have gold . . . Today, age is needy and, as its powers decline, so does its income; but full-blooded youth has wealth as well as vigour. In this decade we witness the second Children's Crusade . . .
>
> (MacInnes 1961, as quoted in Mungham and Pearson 1976)

Sadly, as the corresponding employment situation in the 1980s and 1990s was to prove, despite a tangible improvement in working-class standards of living, this period of prosperity was merely transitory. None the less, Osgerby's (1998) discussion of youth consumption during this period is worth developing in that he manages to portray not only young people's enthusiasm for consumption, but also the way in which young people blended into broader social and economic change. In many respects, the teenager was symbolic of the sorts of social transformations that characterized the 1950s and 1960s which saw a tenuous consumer boom based on the vulnerable economic foundation of short-term credit. But during a period when advertisers were intent on associating their products with the dynamism of youth there was emerging as a result, a new age of hedonistic consumerism among young people (Osgerby 1998). Particularly significant in this respect was the increasingly normalization of the term 'teenager' itself:

> In the image of the 'teenager' post-war mythologies of affluence found their purest manifestation. Taken as the quintessence of social transformation, 'teenagers' were perceived as being at the sharp end of the new consumer culture, distinguished not simply by their youth but by a particular style of conspicuous, leisure-oriented consumption.
>
> (Osgerby 1998: 35)

Young people's consumption patterns were immediate and transitory and therefore had economic implications as well as social ones, but above all the 'teenager' played an ideological role in eroding traditional class boundaries. In effect, young people seemed to represent 'a symbolic foretaste of good times waiting around the corner for everyone' (Osgerby 1998: 35). The implication here, unfounded though it may have been, was that post-war British society was moving towards a new era of classlessness.

Regardless of the class implication of changing patterns of consumption the 1950s and 1960s undoubtedly witnessed a revolution in consumer youth industries most vocally expressed through the growth of pop music which went hand in hand with television programmes such as *Ready, Steady, Go!* in transmitting youth lifestyles through forms of consumption. As Ehrenreich *et al.* (1997) point out, rock 'n' roll became the most potent commodity to enter teen consumer culture. Music provided a vehicle through which young people could express themselves according to their musical taste, alongside the appropriate forms of dress and fashion. In this context, the media played a key role in broadening and popularizing forms of youth consumption that would have been impossible without it (Osgerby 1998).

Fashion clearly played an important role in the emergence of consumer-based lifestyles during the 1950s and 1960s, notably through subcultures such as the Mods who prioritized notions of style and smartness. But an interesting point here is that consumption was equally as liable to have a negative impact on the construction of young people's lives. That is, alternative subcultures, and most notably Rockers, rejected the 'effeminacy' of conspicuous consumption in favour of a sturdy image of masculinity, paradoxically legitimizing dominant ideologies of consumerism by operating within those ideological parameters (Osgerby 1998). But perhaps the most significant point to make in this respect is that, as Ehrenreich *et al.* (1997) argue, consumption appeared to provide young people with a resource which allowed them to solidify their identities separate from both child and adult worlds. No longer obliged to take on the façade of little adults, young people could set about expressing their teenhood through their own products, taste and modes of self-expression.

The commercial expression of teenhood continued throughout the 1970s and 1980s. This cannot be expressed better perhaps than through the qualitative work conducted by Susie Fisher and Susan Holder at the beginning of the 1980s. In the following passage they lucidly express the sorts of responsibilities, tensions and pressures to consume that became characteristic of young people's lives during this period:

money also gives you the freedom to be what you want to be . . . Managing money so you can get what you want isn't play acting in the way that being in the fashion is play acting. It is a real skill. If Joanne can make £3.25 a week stretch to a Pretenders' album, a new skirt and a trip to the cinema, then when she gets paid £50 a week she'll be able to pay the mortgage, eat on Saturdays and take a holiday in Florida.

(Fisher and Holder 1981: 165–6)

It is indeed worth pointing out that regardless of the increased spending power of young people it would be naive to suggest that young people's ability to consume was limitless: far from it. Often, it seems to be the case that the opportunity to dream about consuming, to 'hang out' at shopping centres for example, was more important than the act of consumption itself, precisely because the ability to dream about consumption was grounded on communal ideals about what constituted a consumer culture:

> it's worth explaining what a teenager means by 'shopping'. They may eventually make a purchase, but most of the time they're just looking around, sizing up one thing against another, asking for their mates' opinions, deciding just how much they want to buy it . . . They also get a lot of pleasure first by simply browsing around shops – looking at toiletries, magazines, books, stationery, records, fashion accessories, models, kits, toys, games, sweets etc. The kids felt free to poke around, see what was for sale, try out the testers, browse without being harassed and hustled: 'It's trendy to go to a place like Virgin Records on a Saturday morning – all the punks sit around outside so I really enjoy going there – it's just the getting over the fear of going through the door.'
>
> (Fisher and Holder 1981: 170)

By the 1980s it was almost as if consumerism had emerged as a way of life for young people. Not only did it represent a valuable means of self-expression, but it provided a resource for the construction of everyday life. This was very much a two-way relationship in the sense that youth consumption not only solidified young people's relationships, but it also provided economic benefits. For instance, Côté and Allahar (1996) describe the way in which teenage magazines are dominated by advertising beauty-care products, fashion, clothing and other items designed to enhance young people's appearance and popularity. In discussing the work of Evans *et al.* (1991), Côté and Allahar (1996) point out that while overtly these magazines promote self-improvement they do so by suggesting that conformation to fashion trends (via consumption and more specifically self-beautification) is the only legitimate way of pursuing such an improvement (see Chapter 5).

The more pressing problem as far as young people were concerned was that from the late 1970s onwards and during a period when the

media-driven portrayals of consumer lifestyles were at their most vivid
– and the pressures to conform to modes of consumption as a form of
self-expression were at their most persuasive – in practical and economic
terms, young people were actually more vulnerable than they had been
for decades. As several authors have noted, young people were beginning to experience increasingly extended transitions both into employment and adulthood than was previously the case, thereby undermining
their ability to partake in consumerism as a way of life (see Jones
and Wallace 1992; Roberts 1995). Ironically, in an environment where
the Conservative government was keen to promote an ideology of
consumer sovereignty and enterprise, as symbolized by young upwardly
mobile professionals, or 'yuppies' as they were affectionately known,
and at a time when the pressures to consume were intensified, for a
lot of young people their freedom to consume was becoming in
creasingly constrained. But despite such reservations, young people
emerged as an increasingly important market as the disposability of
their income became increasingly obvious. This was confirmed in
1990 by research carried out by BMRB which found that two-thirds of
15- to 19-year-olds had some form of current bank account (Stewart
1992).

The 1990s were no easier for young people in balancing the contradictory offerings of a consumer culture. Indeed, nowadays the pressures
on young people to consume appear to be in force at an earlier and
earlier age. Gunter and Furnham (1998) have devoted an entire book
to a psychological analysis of the young people's market, pointing out
that young people are socialized as consumers at an early age through
the simple act of parents taking their children grocery shopping, for
instance. Children are 'consumer socialised' not only by their parents,
but also by their peers. Gunter and Furnham report some research conducted by McNeal (1992) in which child consumption was found to be
influenced by peers at the age of seven. The peer-related pressures on
children and young people to consume are clearly massive (see Middleton et al. 1994) and this can have grave financial implications for less
affluent parents struggling to keep pace with the demands of a consumer
culture.

Consumers of the avant-garde

In her discussion of American teenage history Palladino (1996) points
out that young people experiment and that consumption provides the
means by which they can do so. The fact that the American market

alone is ten times the size it was in 1957 is a reflection of how important the youth market is to the economy and, in turn, how important consumption is to young people. Indeed, Gunter and Furnham (1998) note that despite a 15.5 per cent drop in the actual number of teenagers during the 1980s, their spending power increased by nearly 43 per cent (see Tootelian and Gaedeke 1992). Today's teenagers take it for granted that they were 'born to shop' (Starkey 1989; Palladino 1996: xix); the problem being that resource-wise, the ability to shop is easier said than done. Palladino implies, however, that young people's relationship with consumer culture is far from being the radical rebelliousness, which (as I will argue) may have been accurate in the past. Nowadays young people are compelled to find a job and make money in order to belong to the consumer culture which they so fervently crave. Young people are worried about their economic future and as a consequence their relationship with consumption is ever more tenuous and yet ever more fundamental to who it is they are.

Many commentators (e.g. Hendry *et al.* 1993) suggest that it is during their leisure time that young people 'truly become themselves'. With the luxury of being able to prioritize their free time and at a stage in their lives when they have fewer responsibilities than they are ever likely to have, young people are able to establish a distinct realm of their own, what Marsland (1993) describes as 'an island of freedom . . . a sacred bastion of individuality' (p. 108). A Department of Education and Science survey (1983) into young people's lifestyles comes to the conclusion that for many young people how they spend their leisure time is *the* question that constantly remains central to their life experience.

In light of the above discussion it is tempting to concur with Drotner's (1992) contention that young people amount to a sort of 'avant-garde' of consumption in the sense that they appear to be the most pioneering sector of consumers, even going as far as consuming the unconsumable. In other words, they commodify virtually anything. The penchant for second-hand clothing among young people in Britain during the mid-1990s is a good example of this (see McRobbie 1994). It is also worth noting Drotner's (1991) point that young people in the 1990s appear to be preoccupied with creating themselves and therefore have particularly well-developed needs for aesthetic consumption, needs transmitted to them via television and the media for instance. They are indeed, 'the pioneers of consumer society' (Drotner 1991: 49). This reflects a paradoxical situation where young people are increasingly culturally independent in terms of the free time and money at their disposal and yet they are increasingly dependent upon adults economically as a result of delayed transitions into the workplace. This point in itself serves to reiterate the key role played in the construction of social life by the relationship between structure and agency.

One author who has managed to construct a balanced analysis of young people as consumers while touching upon the above debates is Fiona Stewart (1992) who argues that with demographic change the commercial centre of gravity will, in the long term, shift away from young people and towards middle-aged consumers. But regardless of historical trends, Stewart suggests that young people today have a greater degree of autonomy in what they consume than ever before. Sadly, however, young people are having to live in a harsher economic climate than their predecessors. This has led to a reappraisal of young people's values; in a world where consumption is omnipresent young people are essentially conventionally conservative in their everyday approach to life. The fact, in turn, that they live in such an individualistic culture has undermined any notion of the unified nature of youth culture as I implied in Chapter 6. Stewart's (1992) argument is particularly useful in so far as she points out that consumption among young people has become increasingly fragmentary. The status that young people procure from what they consume is not a result of the ability to buy goods in a general sense, but is dependent upon buying goods that are different from what others buy. I tend to diverge from Stewart on this point in that although young people evidently adopt fragmented forms of consumption, they consume in a broader framework dependent upon a cultural capital of consumption which is omnipresent among their friendship circle. They simply cannot afford to consume individualistically. I do, however, agree with Stewart's (1992) suggestion that what characterizes young people in terms of their core values is that, above all, they are being incorporated into the mainstream. For the majority of young people there appears to be very little left for them to rebel against. Give a young person the opportunity to drive his or her first car and he or she will be happy (Veash and O'Sullivan 1997). In this context, young people are independent of mind and yet paradoxically conformist in a world where 'the individual experiences and the influences individuals are exposed to are becoming increasingly homogenous' (Stewart 1992: 224). The question that needs to be asked therefore is: are young people in control of their consumption patterns, or are they being controlled?

Controlled or in control?

The actual spending patterns of young people has become a topic of increasing interest among researchers in recent years. For instance,

Gunter and Furnham (1998), not surprisingly perhaps, found that both male and female teenagers spent most of their money on clothes, records, stereo equipment, entertainment and travel, while in recent years shopping has become a favourite social activity for young people. Gunter and Furnham also found that young people exert considerable secondary influence on their parents' consumption patterns, notably in terms of the aesthetic qualities of the products under consideration. In addition, a lot of research has indicated that brand loyalties formed during childhood have a significant long-term influence on adult purchasing patterns (Gunter and Furnham 1998). But such research raises important questions about the extent to which young people are indeed in control of what they consume. Of particular interest then is Jones and Martin's (1997) suggestion that although on the surface young people appear to have power as consumers, such power can only be considered in the context of broader concerns about their transition to adulthood. Basing their research on the Family Expenditure Survey which incorporates data on over 2,000 young people aged between 16 and 25, Jones and Martin conclude that there is unequal access to consumer goods among young people and that youth consumption is inherently multidimensional. In particular, they point out that leisure spending is an especially important survival strategy for young people in a world where the certainty and boredom of life within the confines of the transitional household is becoming increasingly attractive as an alternative to the uncertainties characterized by the outside world (see Chapter 3). The clear implication here is that young people do not necessarily use consumption as a means of asserting their power, but rather as a means of survival in a society where the extent of the power available to them is increasingly being eroded (Jones and Martin 1997).

The key debate here appears to centre on how far youth consumption is actually 'authentic'. There surely cannot be much doubt that throughout the twentieth century marketers have become increasingly cunning and perceptive as new consumption niches have been established. Thus, the Key Note Market Review (1994) which specifically addresses the nature of youth, describes the 12 to 21 age group as being represented by several discrete markets including school-age children, young earners, young unemployed and students. Given that young people in this age group are experiencing dramatic change physiologically, socially, economically and emotionally, the big question centres on how far marketers actively exploit the fact that young people have to deal with these changes.

In discussing the impact of consumer culture upon the lives of young people there has indeed been a tendency to see young people as a highly vulnerable sector of the population, easily persuaded for instance, by the superficialities of advertising (see Nava and Nava 1990). Many authors have taken a negative viewpoint on the above developments. Jeremy Seabrook (1978) who is worth quoting at some length, goes as far as to suggest that the predominance of commodities in young people's lives is essentially dehumanizing:

> To grow up under the domination of consumer capitalism is to see that part of us which used to belong to society to be colonized, torn away from traditional allegiances, and be hurled, lone and isolated into the prison of the individual's senses. The child tends to be stripped of all social influences but those of the market-place; all sense of place, function and class is weakened, the characteristics of region or clan, neighbourhood or kindred are attenuated. The individual is denuded of everything but appetites, desires and tastes, wrenched from any context of human obligation or commitment. It is a process of mutilation; and once this has been achieved we are offered the consolation of reconstructing the abbreviated humanity out of the things and the goods around us, and the fantasies and vapours which they emit.
>
> (pp. 5–6)

Young people are apparently forced to construct their identities from the parade of images and products that surround them to the extent that they are 'carried off in the fleshy arms of private consumption, and to an unidentified location (fantasy, actually) to be systematically shaped to the products which it will be their duty to want, to compete for and consume' (Seabrook 1978: 98). Indeed, it has been suggested that there is evidence of an increasing emphasis on the construction of a 'feel-good' existence among young people, for they live in a world where all organizations and activities are designed to 'either produce or consume something' (Côté and Allahar: 136). Côté and Allahar see the omnipresence of consumption in young people's lives as providing a means of distracting them from the reproduction of dominant power structures which are in actual fact perpetuating the social impotence of young people. It is also true to say, however, that the temptation to romanticize a mythical time prior to a consumer society, when young people were able to be who they were when they wanted without being controlled by the ravages of consumer products and lifestyles (a view clearly evident in Seabrook's (1978) work), needs to be avoided.

More recently, the realization that young people are, in fact, quite capable of transforming the politics of consumption for their own ends and, in turn, quite capable of establishing a critical stance on what consumer culture has to offer them, has emerged (Willis 1990; Griffin 1993). Willis, in particular, argues:

> People bring living identities to commerce and the consumption of cultural commodities as well as being formed there. They bring experiences, feelings, social position, and social memberships to their encounter with commerce. Hence they bring a necessary creative symbolic pressure, not only to make sense of cultural commodities, but partly through them also to make sense of contradiction and structure as they experience them in school, college, production, neighbourhood, and as members of certain genders, races, classes and ages.
>
> (p. 21)

Consumption is, in effect, *the* arena within which young people express their creativity. Cultural commodities are the raw materials, the catalyst through which young people conduct their cultural affairs. Far from being passive consumers of leisure consumption young people actively participate and negotiate with the goods made available to them (see Frith's (1978) discussion of music buying). Nava and Nava (1990) develop this sort of argument in their discussion of young people as consumers of advertising. They suggest that young people are in fact very discriminating consumers of advertising and that they consume commercials as cultural products in themselves rather than simply as vehicles for selling. From this point of view, young people are more sophisticated consumers than their elders.

Many authors have also commented on the way in which young people use sites of consumption in a reflexive constructive fashion. For instance, Presdee (1990) notes that young people are attracted to shopping malls as 'cathedrals of consumption', often asserting their right to claim space as non-consumers in a consumer-oriented world. Similarly, Langman (1992) argues that mall culture has a particularly influential role as far as young people are concerned, in as much as it provides a hang-out in which they can be free of parental pressure, a community of peers, which ironically confirms to young people the legitimacy of a consumer lifestyle. In effect, malls play the role of harbingers of pseudo-communities, providing a means or focus by which young people are integrated into subsequent life trajectories. Malls give young people the opportunity to contest, reinterpret and mobilize meanings; they provide a source of empowerment through 'hyper-real gratification' (Langman 1992: 60). But the key issue here as far as this book is concerned, and as Langman (1992: 60–1) points out, is that

Adolescent groups with common cultural capital become the socialization agents for, and models of, what Bellah (1985) has termed lifestyle enclaves that reflect current life chances and subcultures of particular consumer tastes which offer identity packages that typically endure through subsequent life careers. But these are really more 'proto-communities' of shared patterns of cultural consumption and communication through shared tastes and fashion than the more traditional forms of community and face-to-face verbal communication.

One of the most informative approaches to the above trends is that of Lopiano-Misdom and De Luca (1997) who present a market research firm's analysis of patterns of youth consumption. From their American perspective they argue that youth culture is currently 'the most resourceful, intellectual and creative generation that we have seen in the past fifty years' (p. xiii). Their vision of young people as consumers is of a heterogeneous group driven by independence and the need to gain respect. Thus, Lopiano-Misdom and De Luca discuss the ways in which some minority forms of consumption such as techno-music have been transferred by young people into the mainstream. At least to some extent then, the market appears to listen to what young people have to say:

> the relationship between consumer industries and the media on the one hand and the teen audience on the other is interactive: the teens respond and the market listens. The relationship is based on consumption, of course, but the interaction encourages creativity and quality in the production of goods and communication, and predictability in the audience. The tendencies to conform are encouraged also by the use of media and consumer information as communication among teens. Shopping as a group entertainment activity is only the last stage of a process by which teens collect and share information on what's in and proceed to adopt a style.
>
> (White 1993: 104)

Similarly, the Key Note Market Review (1994) of the UK youth market emphasizes young people's creative enthusiasm for new technologies. But the irony here is that while eulogizing about the creative energy that lies behind youth consumption, authors such as Lopiano-Misdom and De Luca (1997) who champion the cause of youth consumption, undermine the very creative force which apparently they seek to promote. They call for the commercialization of emerging forms of youth consumption, but by doing so threaten the creative foundations upon which such consumption is based. This then appears to be the essential paradox of youth consumption. Young people use musical styles, fashion and other forms of consumption as a means of constructing who it is they are in the context of proto-communities or lifestyles, but simply by doing so the creative spirit engendered by young people is arguably compromised by the market. Of course, young people can continue to consume cultural commodities in their own ways, but ultimately such consumption has to become subject to the needs of the marketplace. In this sense then, young people can never be completely free as consumers. The relationship between the consumer industries and the media on the one hand and young consumer on the other is creative, as White (1993) points out, but whether or not young people retain the more powerful hand in that situation is a matter for debate.

In this context, Rojek (1989) and Griffin (1993) express the concern that the freedoms young people experience, notably in the context of consumption, are all too often grossly exaggerated by a mind-set that sees young people's leisure time as inherently liberating. Far from being free to choose exactly what they want to do and when, young people are constrained by all sorts of social structures and inequalities. Indeed, many authors have argued that young people's experience of consumption is essentially paradoxical in an environment where economic dependency has been extended, while conversely young people appear to be thrown into the machinations of the marketplace at an earlier and earlier age. The problem is that despite the insecurities associated with young people's lives they amount to an attractive prospect to the marketplace in terms of their current disposable income and their long-term potential as brand-aware consumers, a process exacerbated by the deregulation of credit in the 1980s. As White (1993: 5–6) points out, the media and marketers have exploited this situation to the full in order to amplify the separateness of a youth culture and thereby distinguish the youth market from its adult market counterpart.

To claim young people use consumption purely for their own ends would clearly serve to underestimate the inherently paradoxical nature of consumer lifestyles. For instance, Osgerby (1998) discusses the Casuals, a mainly male group who wore smart designer labels and who were often associated during the 1980s with football hooliganism. He suggests that such smart dress represented two-fingered gestures of defiance which asserted their ability to behave and dress in ways unexpected of a subordinate group. This may have been the case, but by doing so it might equally be argued that such groups simply legitimized the far right market-driven principles of the Conservative government at the time. Young people were living in a world of contradictions where economic empowerment provided benefits if you were prepared to 'get on your bike' as Norman Tebbit once infamously proposed. Alongside this superficial impression of consumer sovereignty there exists a slippery slope between economic independence and insecurity.

As already noted, far from being characterized by rebellion against the dominant values of society, young people often actually positively embrace those values wholeheartedly. In many ways, as the discussion of rave in Chapter 6 illustrated, they have arguably become vehicles for the active expression of the dominant values of society at the end of the twentieth century. This reflects the concomitant trend for sociologists of youth to exaggerate the rebellious nature of young people (see Chapter 1). Furthermore

> There is a tendency to overstate the cultural power of youth in the sphere of consumption . . . Youth-orientated journalism has a vested interest in doing so, to flatter the youthful consumer's powers of musical and fashion discrimination or perhaps, in the more 'serious' forms, to arbitrate on taste, to signify where the action is, in magazines emerging in the 1980s such as *The Face* and its successors.
>
> (McGuigan 1992: 91)

It would be misleading to suggest that all young people throw themselves wholeheartedly and gratuitously into a world of consumerism; Osgerby's (1998) discussion of 'grunge' as angst-ridden disaffection with the insecurities of life is a case in point. But even those subcultures that appear to reject dominant social values do so in such a way as to promote consumerism as a way of life, in this case through the consumption of grunge music and particular styles of baggy dress which ultimately serve to create yet another market niche.

Discussion

What does all this mean for the future of young people as consumers? Gaines (1991) argues that young people are essentially over-consumed. They are disillusioned with what consumption can offer them and are looking for alternatives in a world where disaffection, cynicism and depression are the order of the day. By contrast, Rushkoff (1997) has a far more optimistic view of the future in which 'screenagers', children born into a culture mediated by the television and the computer, are grabbing hold of the opportunities offered to them by a technological consumer-driven society, propelling that society into the future as they do so. In this vision, young people are the gatekeepers of a fragmented and yet manageable world as expressed through their paradoxical relationship with consumption. For example,

> Skateboarders' clothing is . . . extremely tag-conscious, even more conspicuously and meaningfully than in the conventional fashion world. Professional teams are organized under specific labels, and a few skaters have been allowed themselves to be tattooed with their company's logo. Often, rather than just relating the name of the designer, the label promotes a social agenda, however simplistic. Wearing the '*fuct*' label is a statement in itself, and the company's slogan, in blaring self-consciousness, proclaims, 'profanity is profit'.
>
> (Rushkoff 1997: 31)

Reimer (1988), however, in his discussion of the post-materialist hypothesis, concludes that young people react to the nature of contemporary social (and environmental) change in a host of different ways and can therefore be said to reflect sophisticated 'post-modern structures of feeling' (p. 357). In other words, one of the most important things to remember about young people nowadays is that they cannot easily be pigeon-holed, not least because they are constantly treading a peculiarly delicate path between media influence and freedom of choice, a peculiarly delicate path between conformity and individual meaning. The point here, as Widdicombe and Wooffitt (1995) point out, is that conformity and young people's relationship to conformity is not neutral. It represents a highly significant focus for the construction of a young person's identity. White (1993) for instance, discusses the phenomenon of young teenage girls in Japan who travel around in trains for the sole purpose of seeing what fashions are new and how these fashions are interpreted by fellow teenagers. As such, style, and the use of consumer goods to establish a style, appears to represent a very important aspect of young people's lives:

> A very large proportion of the leisure time of young people is indeed devoted to 'putting on the style'. But this is no trivial matter. For it is the outward expression of their self-exploration and testing of alternative identities – which is precisely the developmental task for which young people use their leisure time.
>
> (Marsland 1993: 130)

In effect, young people need a realm in which their role relationships can *feel* relaxed and comfortable and within which the self can be invigorated, regardless of the ideological impact that that realm has on their lives

(Hendry *et al.* 1993). In a world where full participation in adult culture is precluded by social change which has actively extended youth transitions, young people are obliged to develop their own cultures, arguably, in an attempt to find a more meaningful identity. Equally, therefore, consumption could be argued to fit the bill:

> Consumer styles and artifacts come to be perceived as an integral part of [young people's] identities. Participation in markets thus becomes a 'need', so that young people feel they need to be conspicuously sporting the latest styles and show their awareness of the latest trends.
>
> (Jones and Wallace 1992: 119–20)

Young people's roles as pseudo-consumer citizens appears to represent an important aspect of them asserting who it is they are, notably because during the teenage years and beyond, access to consumer markets brings for some the opportunity to experience new freedoms, forms of independence and choice (Jones and Wallace 1992). But it is all too easy to forget that these sorts of freedoms are only attainable when a young person and his or her family's material conditions allow. Young people are, more often than not, as Jones and Wallace argue, at least partially dependent consumers, a fact which reflects above all the changing nature of not only youth lifestyles but also youth transitions in general. The fact that many young people quite often do not even have their essential needs met in terms of food, water and shelter, should not therefore be forgotten. It is therefore essential to identify the polarization that exists between those young people who can consume and those who can only dream about consuming.

Osgerby (1998) suggests, however, that in one respect at least, the bubble of youth consumption has recently been burst. The sorts of economic processes that were taking effect at the end of the 1980s and the beginning of the 1990s (see Chapter 3), created a situation where larger numbers of young people were dependent upon the welfare state, or quite often on miniscule incomes from highly insecure 'McJobs'. Arguably in this context, manufacturers and marketers began to look to alternative markets. In effect, the commercial youth market might be said to have begun to be eclipsed by new non age-specific growth areas including film, fashion and music. This much may be at least partially true. The credibility of youth as a market in its own right has begun to be questioned. Cultural industries such as television, film, music and advertising began to gear themselves less to generational categories than to particular attitudes and lifestyles (Osgerby 1998). In effect, taste rather than age became the defining feature of youth culture, and the commercial potential of the youth market, and the meanings young people could invest in consumerism were actually immeasurably expanded, in the sense that 'youth' came to mean more than simply a particular age group, but a lifestyle in its own right.

There are all sorts of factors involved in an assessment of young people as consumers, such as gender, ethnicity, disability, sexual orientation, geographical location, and social class (see Morrow and Richards 1996). In this context, as discussed above, Paul Willis' (1990) influential discussion of the culturally creative experience of young people as consumers provides a valuable insight into the nature of youth consumption. His attempt to come to terms with the meanings with which individuals endow consumer culture represented a significant advance in the field of youth studies. However, Willis (1990) undoubtedly over-estimated the degree to which young people can assert their own agency within the frameworks that consumption provides. Young people do not have the advantage of complete freedom of access and cannot freely construct meanings. Youth consumption is far more complex than this sort of approach tends to imply. Consumption is not always an ordered and easily explained activity, as this chapter has illustrated. But lessons can be learned from Willis' situated analysis of young people's experiences of consumption and in this context:

> It is important to consider how various groups of young women (and men) are represented in specific contexts as consumers, and especially as disordered consumers, and the ways in which such representations and the associated regime management and treatment are gendered, sexualized, racialized and class-specific.
>
> (Griffin 1997: 16)

Focusing more specifically on the relationship between the construction and management of 'troubled teens', apparently subject to specific disorders of consumption and transition, Griffin identifies many young people as 'disordered consumers in racially-structured patriarchal capitalist societies' (p. 5). She goes on to point out that rising youth unemployment and increasingly complex global cultures and technological forms have actively undermined some of the certainties which previously formed a basis for an assessment of youth cultural styles.

Although youth lifestyles have come to the fore and although 'youth' represented a major target of those cultural industries seeking to expand their markets, it does not necessarily follow that life for young people represents a consumerist nirvana where age no longer limits the horizons of their consumerist lifestyles. Consumption may well provide the raw materials for young people's lifestyles at the end of the twentieth century, but those raw materials are neither democratic nor free of the ideological dimensions of consumer capitalism. Above all, the problem might well be that consumer culture and the dominance of the market have insured that young people are constantly surrounded by ideological symbols of consumerism and have therefore, at least superficially, constructed them as consumer citizens. However, the promise of consumerism is rarely matched by the reality. Indeed, many authors have noted that young people rarely use the diversities provided by the market and that as consumers young people are actually becoming increasingly conservative, almost as if the market has hypnotized them into a social and political inertia (McCabe 1980). But ultimately, this sort of a suggestion may well be somewhat extreme, not least when you consider the fact that so many young people simply cannot tap into the consumerist lifestyles that surround them.

The point is that even if a young person cannot consume, the desirous qualities of consumption will still quite possibly play a strong part in the construction of their lifestyle. The world in which young people live at the end of the twentieth century is characterized by diversity and disadvantage, provoking Griffin (1997: 18) to ask the following rather chilling question: 'What if the bait (steady job, nice things, lovely home/car/baby/husband) fails to materialize at all?' The rose-tinted world of consumerism is not always an option for young people in a world full of paradox and uncertainty. Indeed, young people may have been socialized into being 'conspicuous consumers' as Jones and Wallace (1992) point out, but they do not necessarily have the resources to take on such a responsibility. Consumer lifestyles offer young people a world of riches apparently available to one and all. Indeed, Urry (1990) describes the act of consumption as an act of citizenship. However, ultimately, young people do not have either the stability or the resources to operate as fully-fledged citizens of a consumer society because that society offers all the temptation without the secure economic and social foundations upon which such stability can be built. The pervasive image many of us may have of young people – that of the confident and apparently affluent consumer calling his or his friends from a highly fashionable bar or from a street corner – may not be an entirely accurate one. Many young people have been 'liberated' by the global opportunities provided by consumerism, but many have not. It is the sociologist of youth's responsibility to balance the pros and cons of consumerism as a way of life (Miles 1998). To this end, in the next chapter I will present a piece of my own research which attempts to address, empirically, the nature of young people's consumer lifestyles.

Recommended reading

Gunter, Barrie and Furnham, Adrian (1998) *Children as Consumers: A Psychological Analysis of the Young People's Market*. London: Routledge.
  An exhaustive and informative book which illustrates the psychological factors underlying young people's emergence as consumers.
Osgerby, Bill (1998) *Youth in Britain Since 1945*. Oxford: Blackwell.
  Young people's role as consumers is highlighted as representing a fundamental factor in their relationship with social change.
Palladino, Grace (1996) *Teenagers: An American History*. New York: Basic Books.
  An American discussion of the emergence of youth which is particularly useful in highlighting the significance of the youth market.
Stewart, Fiona (1992) The adolescent as consumer, in J. C. Coleman and C. Warren-Anderson (eds) *Youth Policy in the 1990s: The Way Forward*. London: Routledge, pp. 203–26.
  A useful summary of the nature of young people's spending patterns and the active ways in which they consume.

8
CONSUMER LIFESTYLES
IN CONTEXT

This book has attempted to outline some of the key issues arising in young people's lives at the beginning of the twenty-first century. The suggestion is that consumer lifestyles play a key role in young people's everyday navigation of an ever-changing world. In turn, consumption provides the primary arena within which young people's lifestyles are changing. The highly flexible nature of consumption and the diversity of ways in which meanings can be endowed in consumer goods make it an ideal arena for the construction of identities through lifestyles. In effect, consumption provides an arena within which young people can be, or at least can attempt to be, themselves. In order to illustrate this point, and in order to establish an empirically based flavour of what constitutes young people's lifestyles at the end of the twentieth century, in this chapter I will present an extended analysis of a piece of research that looks directly at these issues.

This chapter illustrates the benefit of conducting research that is more concerned with the active ways in which young people conduct their lifestyles than the more rigid subcultural or structural analyses that have tended to characterize a lot of work in this area. At the same time it is important to point out that young people are not entirely free to construct their own identities or lifestyles, and that these are the product of a two-way relationship between structure and agency. In this context, the realization that consumption plays a key role in the construction of young people's lifestyles leads to my underlying contention: namely that young people's lifestyles can only be understood as active meaningful constructions and that these constructions are closely bound up with the formation of young people's identities. The construction of identities is in turn bound up with the concomitant rapidity of social and cultural change as expressed through social structures. This combines to create a heady cocktail. To this end, Yardley and Honess (1987) point out that

> The changes heralded in childhood point to adolescents' newly emerging capacity to construct rather than simply 'find' meanings. This, in conjunction with considerable biological, social and personal change, underlies the continuing significance of the 'teenage' years for the consolidation of a sense of self.
>
> (pp. xv–xvi)

Consumption could therefore be said to play a particularly important role in constructing young people's lifestyles 'as part . . . of the repertory with which users carry out the operations of their own' (DeCerteau 1984: 31). Indeed, I would go as far as to suggest that the meanings which young people endow in their lives as consumers represents a fundamental building block in the construction of who it is they are. Young people do not construct their identities directly through what they consume, but consumption plays an important role as a vehicle for the construction of young people's lifestyles and it is largely within this context that their identities are constructed.

The research I will discuss in this chapter was conducted in Huddersfield and Glasgow, in the mid to late 1990s. The initial aim of the research was to address the relationship between consumption and the construction of young people's identities. However, the strategic decision to focus on the meanings which young people invest in what they consume, soon brought with it a wealth of telling empirical data about the nature of young people's lifestyles and it is that material which I will concentrate on here. It is important to point out that I am not claiming that the data presented will prove anything about the significance of consumer lifestyles in young people's lives, but rather that it will provide a flavour of what constitutes those lifestyles and why they are so important in understanding who young people are.

The project consisted of a three-stage research model which deployed the following methods as an empirical basis for the research:

1 A series of group interviews.
2 A participant observation in a sports shop.
3 A Consumer Meanings Lifestyle Questionnaire.

Stages 2 and 3 were more concerned with the specific ways in which young people endowed consumer goods with meanings. This material has been discussed in greater detail elsewhere (Miles 1996, 1997). In this chapter I will therefore concentrate on data collected during the first phase of the research which was more concerned with coming to terms with what constituted 'youth lifestyles' in general.

A series of group interviews were undertaken with young people aged between 16 and 20 years of age. A total of 30 respondents, ten in each group, were interviewed according to the three-stage interview process, two stages of which I will discuss below. The gender balance of these groups was relatively equal and all students were recruited from local further education colleges. It is also worth pointing out that the members of the individual groups did know each other. This made discussion within the groups much more natural. Each of the total of nine interviews was approximately one hour long. All my respondents were guaranteed confidentiality. This was important as during the course of the three interview stages I became reasonably familiar with the attitudes and occasionally, the personal lives, of the respondents concerned.

The first of the three interview stages was intended to provide an environment within which young people could discuss general issues as to the nature of their consumer lifestyles. As such, I did not go into the interviews with a strict interview schedule in hand, but rather intended to provide a forum within which young people could discuss what they felt was appropriate within a broad discussion concerning young people, consumer lifestyles and identities.

The second of the group interviews was more 'focused'. This session was concerned with the ease with which young people associated different 'types' of people with different consumer goods and lifestyles. Were there common ideas as to the sorts of things a rapper, a student, a smart dresser, a heavy, or a 'sunshine boy' would buy? If so, what implications might this have for the identities of young consumers and for the influence of consumer culture on young people's lifestyles?

I presented my focus groups with photographs taken from youth magazines of five teenagers, each of which could be described loosely as being one of the five 'types' above. These specific 'types' were chosen because, as a collective, they represented what appeared to be a reasonable pictorial representation of a cross-section of young people's lifestyles. To aid my respondents in their task, these 'types' were assigned names. A discussion was then generated about what would happen if the focus group members were to change their images and come into college dressed in the appropriate fashion. My groups were then presented with a collage of 26 separate consumer goods, ranging from a hi-fi down to a bottle of beer. The collage consisted of goods that appear to be aimed at the youth market and were chosen for their diversity. However, in addition, there were also items similar to one another in order to see how discriminating young people were about design variations in consumer goods. My respondents were asked to decide *as a group* which of the five people would buy which of the consumer goods. A volunteer was then asked to write the group's decision on the collage. This was then used as a springboard for a discussion about image, consumer goods, lifestyles and identity. Finally, my group members were asked to identify which of the goods they, as an individual, would purchase, given reasonable resources, in order to identify the extent of commonality between the tastes of a given group of teenage consumers.

The third of my three focus group interviews was specifically concerned with data obtained from a particular psychological research tool, namely Personal Construct Psychology (Kelly 1955). This was concerned with the ways in which young people endowed meanings and what this said about the ways in which they constructed their identities. I will not discuss this data in detail here as it is less relevant to a broader discussion of youth lifestyles (see Miles 1997). In the following section I propose to discuss briefly the findings collected during the first two phases of my focus group interviews and how they might, at least in a preliminary fashion, enlighten an understanding of youth lifestyles at the turn of the century. My intention, therefore, is to construct a qualitative picture of the role which consumption, in particular, may or may not play in young people's lifestyles. At this stage, I want, as far as possible, for young people to speak for themselves.

Phase 1

One point that was soon established was that consumption clearly plays an important role in the construction of young people's lifestyles. This became clear in my first interview in which I gave the young people the opportunity to discuss what factors currently played an important role in constructing who it is they were. I began the interview by asking my respondents what five leisure activities they had taken part in during the course of the previous week and to rank them in order of importance. This was intended to encourage my respondents to consider the impact of consumer lifestyles in their lives (although I didn't discuss 'consumer lifestyles' directly, as the rather more abstract nature of that discussion may have been problematic). The young people concerned clearly felt that shopping had a significant role to play as a leisure activity in their lives. Moving on to the more general discussion of shopping that ran through my focus groups, opinion was divided. Whereas some of my respondents saw shopping as 'just something you do', others saw it is having a more important role,

> Darren: It's important to me. I just like doing it. I don't know. I just like getting out and seeing stuff.

The difficulty that people have in actually explaining the importance that shopping and thus consumption has for them in the construction of their everyday lives is a pertinent point. What was of more interest, however, was the fact that on two occasions during my interviews respondents mentioned how important it was for them to come away after a shopping spree with 'something to show for it'.

> Jack: Yeah, you walk around Leeds and you don't really see owt you like and you come home and you're thinking, that were a real waste of time. If you buy something, you're thinking yeah, this has been really worthwhile this. It's been a good day. It's like incentive really.
>
> Marlene: I just buy something for the sake of it.
>
> Interviewer: Would that happen then? You come to the end of your trip and think, aaahhh this has been a waste of time I'd best buy something.
>
> Darren: Occasionally. Once or twice.
>
> Marlene: I'd get annoyed that I ain't got nowt.
>
> Darren: And you get home and think, Christ, why did I get this?
>
> Marlene: You get a good feeling if you walk back with something. If you go out willing to buy something and you come back without anything, then you're thinking, oh my God!

It might be argued that young consumers feel that shopping is somehow a frivolous and wasteful activity unless actively substantiated by an end-product. That, in effect, if you fail to buy something, you are demeaning yourself, you are wasting time and effort, without anything to show for it. You are, in effect, not fulfilling your role as a citizen of consumer culture. On the other hand, if you do manage to purchase something, you are actively contributing to who you are as a person and how you relate to broader social structures and relationships.

Throughout these discussions it was clear that money and the access to resources which a consumer lifestyle demands were a constant pre-occupation for young people. It is all well and good discussing the consumption habits of young people, but without recognizing the finite restrictions on their resources, any discussion of this sort can only be misleading.

> *Louise*: I can't buy what I want, I can only buy what I can afford. If I could buy what I wanted I wouldn't be stuck for choice. But I've got to keep it to a certain price range.

In this context, the young people I interviewed appeared to engage very closely with consumer culture, but did so in a considered and sober fashion. Members of my focus groups exhibited a strong awareness of financial matters. Far from being a trivial matter, spending money was clearly something that justified a lot of thought on the part of my respondents, to the extent that several mentioned how much better they felt about spending money they had earned, as compared to money they were given by their parents,

> *Justine*: Depends on how you got your money as well. Like if you had to work for it, it feels better, than if someone just gave you the money. It's just too easy that way.

All three of my groups were asked how they would spend £50 if I were to give it to each of them. Over half of them said that they would save it, reflecting how responsible they *have* to be in the current economic climate. This emphasis on economy was a recurring theme,

> *Paul*: People tend to go for economy at our age I think actually. As long as it looks good and you like it then I think it's all right.
>
> *Gary*: Doc Marten's are expensive but I've got a pair that I've had for five or six years.
>
> *Reshma*: With Docs they don't wear out that quickly.
>
> *Paul*: Yeah, you can get 'em re-soled and everything. They're really tough. You can get the imitations from Dolcis and the stitching comes out within two weeks. So I wouldn't waste my money.

So, far from the image of young consumers as being carefree and footloose, they seem, certainly in their purchasing decisions, to be very sensible. In reality, they cannot afford to be otherwise,

Justine: There's no way you can just decide I'm gonna start dress-
ing like this and then go out and buy everything. It'd take
yer weeks and weeks to buy one outfit, let alone a whole
wardrobe.

Any discussion of shopping and consumption needs to be aware of these
sorts of concerns. Teenage consumers have to make very careful decisions about the pros and cons of particular items. Having said that,
many are also very aware of the significance of money in contemporary
culture and fully embrace the world of consumerism which surrounds
them,

Gary: We live in a capitalist society though. Money's bound to be
important to us. I mean everybody's out to get as much
money as they possibly can. Give as little away as possible
really.

Indeed, it would be fair to say, and this was further highlighted
during the visual exercises conducted in the second phase, that only
one member of the three groups showed any reluctance at all to become
fully embroiled in the culture of consumerism. All but this one
exception showed a strong desire for consumer goods and never
questioned whether or not this was a desirable or legitimate state of
affairs. Only Elizabeth, in advocating the farm-based lifestyle of her
family, expressed any distaste for consumer goods. The fact that consumer culture generally goes unquestioned, that the ideologies it prof-
fers are embraced wholeheartedly, can only further emphasize how
important it is for the sociologist to come to terms with the subtleties
involved in the construction of consumer lifestyles. On the other hand,
the sociologist must not imply that the influences of consumer culture
are universal.

However, there does appear to be considerable evidence to suggest
that the way in which young people embrace consumerism appears to
be tied up very much to the question of confidence and the need to
belong. The following exchange lucidly illustrates this point:

Tony: If you're walking down the street in Leeds and everyone's
your age and you're wearing something totally different.
You'll be thinking, you know, is everybody looking at
me?
Shannon: But the thing is, if you really feel comfortable in those
clothes and you really like those clothes you wouldn't
feel that way.

Mandy: But if something like that became fashion and everyone started wearing it, you'd probably end up wearing it.

Tony: I'm forever buying stuff just because I've seen it on someone else, I try it on and see if it looks good on me. Then you buy it. It might look rubbish on you, but everybody's wearing it so . . .

Young people appear to use consumer culture as a resource. How peers perceive an individual as a fellow consumer is important, but this would not necessarily determine a young person's choice of consumer goods. In this context, it might well be argued that young people are more than simply 'consumer dupes'. Consumer lifestyles are not all-important, they actively relate to other aspects of young people's lives. Some of my respondents went to great lengths to stress the importance to them of family life, but often went short of saying that their families directly impacted in any influential way on who they were,

Frank: I respect me family. But they don't influence me in any way. I'll ignore most . . . If they knew what I did they'd probably throw me out and never speak to me again but . . .

Above all then, what appears to be the most fundamental influence on young people's lives, as far as they are concerned at least, are their peers. There was considerable evidence to suggest that friendship plays a key role in influencing how young people perceive themselves; indeed, you might argue that consumer lifestyles provide young people with a means to an end.

Interviewer: So talking about friends. How important do you think your friends are to how you are as a person? Do your friends like have a big influence on you or . . .

David: Yeah. They're the most important thing to us.

Interviewer: In what way do you sort of influence you?

David: Whenever you go out. You never go out down town by yourself. Well I never do anyway. Never once been down a night club by meself. Friends are always with me. I mean friends are important aren't they? And it's always the same group of friends, just about.

Jack: I think the way you dress is related to who your friends are. What kind of music you listen to.

This, in turn, can be closely related to what I will say subsequently about the cultural capital of consumption and how it is that friends play an important role in teenagers prioritizing consumption as a means of expression in contemporary society. Teenagers are keen to remain in favour and do so partly through the consumption of mutually accept-able consumer goods, not least music and clothing. Apparently, friend-ship groups play at least some role as arbiters of identity, in that they seem to actually provide a context, a set of parameters, if you like, within which teenagers construct their identities.

Darren: They talk to yer. They can give you confidence or they can take it away I think.

Jack: Say if you go out with a load of mates and they all decide to pick on you that night and you're gonna take crap all night so you're not gonna be confident. But if you're getting along with all the others all right and you're part of a social group then you're gonna feel really good, so you've got more confidence.

The general feeling among my respondents was that though friends were a strong influence in their lives, there is no reason why members of a social group should have identical interests. However, they certainly have at least some influence, not least when it comes to consumer goods,

Ruth: If you go around with people for a long enough time you're bound to end up like them. Not exactly like them, but you'll end up with some of their characteristics, and they'll end up with some of yours.

Martin: If they find something new they like, you sometimes find you like it as well.

It is probably fair to say that friends do play an important part in how teenagers develop as individuals, in all sorts of ways, other than in terms of consumption,

Reshma: But your friends; they don't really like you for what you wear innit. It's just what you are inside really. It's if you can get on and stuff like that. Like with my friend, I knew her at Junior School and everything and then she went to High School, and you know, been to there for about three years. You know, she's a raver. She's out every single night. She's pissed and she's . . . You know. I ain't nothing like that but we still get on.

In particular then, the use of consumer culture as currency in peer con-texts is important to young people, particularly when you consider the question of branding.

Phil: Yeah, they [brand names] give you confidence and that. If you like what you're wearing, if you think you've spent a lot of money on it like, it gives you a lot of confidence.

Andrew: It shows you've a bit of class as well I think if you start wearing name brands.

Interviewer: But why should a name brand be better than something like . . .

Maggie: It's like that purple Timberland jumper you've got [looks at Jack]. Ticket's on inside, so you can't see it anyway.

Jack: Yeah. But you can tell it's a class jumper though.

Jeff: Yeah, but as Darren says, you know yourself.

But it is not purely the fact that friends perceive you in a certain way, as a result of your wearing a particular brand, though this is, of course, important, and is no doubt more important to some teenagers than to others; but the Timberland example illustrates that the significance of the brand name can go further than that. This particular respondent feels better as a result of wearing a brand name, despite the fact that name is not displayed. The confidence gained from that name is not, arguably, a mere result of external influences, that is the meanings applied to it by peers, but such confidence is also 'internal', in that the individual gets a personal sense of satisfaction by wearing what is perceived to be a quality identity-forming product. That product has, in effect, been legitimized by the consumer culture that surrounds the individual and he or she is, in turn, legitimized as a result. The influence of peers in purchasing decisions is important, but so is the individual's perception of how the product concerned fits in to how he or she is as a person in a wider cultural context.

Interviewer: So is it important what your friends think of what you're buying then?

Jason: It's not really what you're buying. It's what they think of you. It kind of comes through in what you're buying.

Interviewer: So are you saying in some way what you buy reflects who you are then?

Jason: Well, partially yes. Well in some things. Not really in food or something like that. But if you're buying clothes or records it reflects on yourself.

Joanna: You want your friends to like it. But it wouldn't affect my decision. I'd want them to like it but if they didn't, I'd buy it anyway.

It can therefore be argued that young consumers are more than mere 'dupes'. That is, they do have at least some degree of critical distance as Willis (1990) argues, and their consumer choices are not completely dominated by peer pressure. Such critical distance was illustrated by many of my respondents who expressed some dissatisfaction with various aspects of consumerism:

Veronica: Yeah, like when Miss Selfridge came to town I was like thinking 'oh yeah!' and then you walked in and it's rubbish. It's useless. It's like what they've got is just exactly the same as what they've got next door in Top Shop or . . . You know . . .

Julie: And I think manufacturers try to exploit people when they're young. Because they see people who are famous on the telly wearing all this gear and stuff or some gorgeous girl or something and they think I'll have to have that. And they aim at people who are younger because they think they are more vulnerable and that sort of thing.

Simon: I think kids have always been acquisitive. It's just that somebody has latched onto that. Somebody's actually started making the products for them to buy. More and more. It started in the sixties really didn't it. I think. Or the fifties. Young people had money so people started making products for them. I mean it's now gone to its extr . . . Well, it's gone further along. And I think as a society we've become more acquisitive anyway. I mean you meet people . . . the latest thing is camcorders. You know. You walk down the street and people rush out with a camcorder.

Phase 2

The role that friends play in the context of the cultural capital of consumption was more forcibly illustrated during the second stage of group interviews. My respondents appeared able to make the tiniest discriminations between similar items, often according to specific brand-names and were easily able, as a group, to agree upon such discriminations.

They would, for instance, seek clarification as to the brand-name of a particular item, the training shoes, or the hi-fi, for example, and base their decision upon that piece of information, immediately collating a brand with an image of a consumer.

In addition, subtle discriminations were made between similar items. For instance, two rucksacks were featured on the collage which was presented to my respondents. Despite being divided into three distinct groups, my respondents designated the rucksacks, broadly speaking, to the same people (Emma, Jay, Jackie, Gary or Simone) depicted in the photographs; they also broadly agreed that, as individual rucksacks, they would appeal to *different* people. What became immediately obvious was that young people have a well-developed ability to label fellow consumers according to specific criteria, criteria they have apparently learnt as a result of being exposed to the wares of consumer culture and the mass media, and as a result of being party to the cultural capital of consumption (Bourdieu 1984). Each of the four groups came up with very similar interpretations of which consumer goods the five people in my pictures might buy. Though it was deemed inappropriate to look at this material statistically inasmuch as it concerned the negotiations of only three groups, in fact the three groups concerned matched 16 of the 26 items with the photographs of the same person (Emma, Gary, Jackie, Jay or Simone). The exercise seemed to come very naturally to all my respondents. The fact that young consumers find it relatively easy to construct an image of what sort of person somebody is, through putting together a jigsaw of consumer goods, would imply that as far as teenage consumers are concerned, consumer lifestyles are strong indicators of what a person is actually like.

All three focus groups located the items displayed with comparative ease and each was quick to come to a consensus. When asked how far they felt the exercise was an easy thing to do, the general opinion, was yes, that it was, but only to an extent,

> *Gordon*: Yeah, you can associate but you don't know if you're right 'cos a lot of people don't wear what you think they would. Me for instance, I like rave, but I like Heavy Metal and stuff as well. You can't tell what people like and don't like.
> *Paul*: It's what's underneath that counts.
> *Gordon*: That's right. Yeah.

Though my respondents acknowledged that it was an impossible task to accurately associate particular consumer goods with pictures of individuals, and thereby draw an accurate picture of what those people are like, they did find it easy to generalize to this end. Their experience of consumer culture was such that they were able to make judgements about individuals according to the clothing they wore. Clearly, when constructing their images of the five individuals they were using the consumer goods on display as a means of expressing who those people were. It was not just a case of guessing what individual items which person would buy, but more importantly they were constructing an overall picture of what a person was like according to the goods he or she might purchase. Thus, my respondents made inferences about the personalities, indeed the identities of the young people in the pictures. This is related to the suggestion that a paradoxical relationship exists between aspects of personal individuality and communal conformity. Gordon, for instance, inadvertently acknowledged the implications of consumer culture, and thereby the limitations of individuality by 'pigeon-holing' one of the people photographed as

> a sunshine boy. That's one of my categories. I have me own categories of how people dress. He's what I call a sunshine boy.

Though he professed himself to be unique, Gordon still employed the cultural capital of consumption as a frame of reference to distinguish between other 'types' of consumer. He acknowledges the existence of consumers who can be identified as following the same trend, but cannot address his own position according to the same criteria.

> *Gordon*: It's easy to associate the actual characters. You know, when they dress like this. But nobody dresses the same all the time.
> *Paul*: But you do.
> *Gordon*: Yeah. I know, but *I'm* different.

Two of the photos used, those of Jay (the sunshine boy) and Emma, who were both dressed in conservative summery clothing, were soon labelled by one of my focus groups as 'health freaks'. Gary and Jackie on the other hand, dressed in their leather jackets and jeans, were quickly marked down as 'music loving drinkers'.

Within this broad agreement, individuals were perfectly prepared to make judgements about the people photographed purely according to what they wore. This was something that my respondents agreed was generally true of real life, say for instance, if you met somebody new.

> *Interviewer*: If it's the first day at college do you think you'd be making judgements about people according to what they were wearing?

All:	Yeah.
Marlene:	That's the first thing you see about 'em. That's before you talk.
Paul:	You shouldn't make judgements against 'em but you do.
Tony:	Everybody does.
Carmen:	Yeah, you know what they're like by their clothes don't yer. Like Docs and a long tie-dye skirt and that, and red hair. You know that they're Gothic don't yer.

Again, while talking about their own consumption habits and their own identities, my respondents talked very much in terms of their individual preferences. Yet, when talking about others they regularly fall back on communal themes. Brand-names came to the fore again in this context.

Interviewer:	You mentioned brand-names. Are brand-names important to people your age?
Jackie:	Can be. Some groups. Depends what you like to wear. Like there's set clothes where it's all names, Reebok, Nike and all sportswear.
Rebecca:	There's the sports and there's the designer and they tend to come in two groups. And you have the designer group, Calvin Klein and stuff like that . . . those sort of names and then you've got sporty type people.

Julie's comments gave this emphasis on brands a more critical edge, while illustrating the pervasiveness of consumer culture, and hence of consumer lifestyles, in young people's lives:

Julie:	It depends what you're into. Like with clothes and stuff. There are some people who avoid labels because they don't wanna go out with people with labels or they're not gonna look like everybody else and that's just as bad as the people who are going out buying the labels.

My respondents appeared to perceive others in terms of their belonging to a particular group of consumers, which adopts well-known styles of dress, and indeed, attitudes, or in terms of being a particular 'type' of consumer. When talking about their own lifestyles these youth cultural characteristics are forgotten and only their own 'personal' style is remembered.

Lorraine:	When we were at school there were a group of girls that wouldn't wear anything but Levi's. Anything that had

> Levi's on they had it. There was a group of girls like that. And it was obviously very important to them, but nobody else cared . . . It's just like really important the way you dress. You can tell 'cos they all dress in the same sort of style. So obviously they've chosen their friends because they look good or because of the way they look, but there's others who it just doesn't matter to.

Many of my respondents felt strongly that they were able to buy, and in particular, wear, exactly what they wanted to be free of pressures of any kind. This is apparently part of maturing as a teenager.

Paul: You just wear what you want, don't yer?
Don: There was more pressure at school. Fifth form at school. It's not as bad now.
Paul: You don't care at all now. You just wear what you want, don't yer?
Caroline: I think everyone's got personal choice, ain't they.

When it came to the part of the exercise where each member of the group identified which consumer goods he or she would purchase given reasonable resources, the results were more diverse. For example, only two items were not chosen by anybody in one of my focus groups. Only the hi-fi was chosen by the majority of my respondents. Otherwise, everybody picked an individualistic sample of goods. Again, this appears to reiterate a point highlighted throughout my group interviews; namely that when discussing their own relationship with consumer goods young people see those goods as being used in highly individualistic and personal ways. And yet, paradoxically, far from young people having considerable disagreements as to who might consume what as a result of this individuality, they appear, in fact, to have highly honed skills of perception about who 'should' consume what. This might well be taken to reinforce my point about young consumers seeing *themselves* as being individually unique and choosing the goods they liked accordingly. In turn, this may explain why consumer lifestyles are so important to young people. In a time of constant personal and social change, consumer lifestyles let them feel that they belong, while retaining a sense of their individuality. In effect, consumer lifestyles represent a means of coping with processes of individualization (see Chapter 4).

Clearly, the meanings with which young people endow consumer goods are highly complex. The contention here is that though what young people say about what they consume and why provides an invaluable framework for conceptualizing the relationship between consumption and identity, this can only begin to be established within a broader critical context. There is no doubt, and I would suggest that the above data speaks for itself in this respect, that young people are quite often discerning consumers. They are not, as Willis (1990) so rightly points out, mere dupes but use consumption in constructive ways. However, these constructions must be understood in the context of the relationship between structure and agency. Young consumers cannot be *pure* agents in any real sense.

What can be noted at this stage is the fact that there appears to be considerable evidence to suggest that the teenage consumer creates some sort of equilibrium between his or her concern as to what others think, and his or her own meanings.

> *Darren*: It's a combination of all things. You wanna buy something you like, you feel comfortable in, and you feel others are gonna like.

What is fundamentally important is that an underlying contradiction can be identified between the critical distance teenagers adopt and the fact that they often fail to acknowledge the fact that they are part of the constraints of consumer culture. As far as most of my respondents are concerned, everybody else but themselves is a victim of consumer lifestyles. A particular comment by one of my respondents illustrates this point well.

> *Gordon*: I've had a quiff for the last five years. Nobody else has. I've never been bothered about it. I started when I was about fifteen. I've never bothered about following anybody else.

Later in the discussion Gordon reiterated this point:

> I didn't get a quiff just to impress everybody because most people don't even like it.

This sort of feeling that individuals are able to sit back and critically reflect on the 'consumer sheep' that surround them is something that pervaded all my groups. Ironically, Gordon was particularly critical of another member of the group.

> *Ian*: Five of us right and we all had our heads shaved at the same time and we all wear the same kind of clothes and we listen to the same kind of music. We all do the same sort of things of a night. We've all tried thieving at one point or another. Things like that.

Catherine:	Don't you think that's just going for someone like a clone.
Gordon:	Do you all speak like this: 'Baaaa.'
Ian:	We don't do exactly the same things . . .
Reshma:	It depends on the individual I think. Because if you can get on with everyone then you can go round with different people.
Caroline:	Yeah, but to get on with them then you've gotta like the same things anyway obviously ain't yer . . .
Gordon:	I get on fine with my girlfriend and I don't like any of the stuff she likes. The only thing we like together is the Smiths. I mean I can't stand the same programmes on TV as she does. She likes all the soaps and I hate them. She listens to blumming ravey music some of the time and I hate it.

Gordon fails to come to terms with the fact that he too is subject to the influence of consumerism and consumerist lifestyles. He does not acknowledge that by adopting his fifties image he is doing as much to 'follow the sheep' as his friend Ian. The paradox lies in the fact that young people often appear to be convinced that they as individuals are able to be unique, that they can choose who they are as a person and choose to opt out of mainstream culture. This paradox is well explained by Simmel (1957: 307):

> Whoever consciously avoids following the fashion does not attain the consequent sensation of individualization through any real individual qualification, but rather through mere negation of the social example. If obedience to fashion consists in imitation of such an example, conscious neglect of fashion represents similar imitation . . . The man [*sic*] who consciously pays no heed to fashion accepts its forms just as much as the dude does, only he embodies it in another category, the former in that of exaggeration, the latter in that of negation.

By opting, in Gordon's case, to become part of 50s culture and despite the personal satisfaction he garners in this context, Gordon can do little more than reaffirm the powerful ideological influence of consumerism. The illusion of choice apparently makes consumption a powerful player in the construction of identities through consumer lifestyles. The fact is that the extent of personal choice is highly constructed. Young consumers are not able to choose the goods they buy off a clean slate, for that slate is already cluttered by the choices that have already been made by their peers and by the producers. Teenage consumers only have personal choice in the context of the parameters laid down for them by the cultural industries and thus consumer lifestyles can never be entirely unique. A popular t-shirt among teenagers during the mid-1990s was one with a prominent slogan that reads 'Demand the right to be unique'. By wearing that t-shirt young consumers may have felt that they were being unique, that they were making a statement. Ultimately, however, that statement was being made by thousands of other teenagers, all of whom were locked into the same paradoxical system of meanings. However, the point here is that young people are fully conversant with both the pervasiveness and the limitations of a consumer lifestyle, and are prepared to live with such limitations for the everyday benefits it provides.

> *Jennifer*: I think because shopping is seen as where the youth culture, a lot of the youth culture lies from the things that spring up from that. Like pop music and things. It's all linked in to fashion, clothes, things like that. Whereas . . . I wasn't living thirty years ago . . . Where I would imagine thirty years ago you saw identity more in your local community and you maybe didn't stray too far out of your local community.

By adopting a group format interview in the above context, I was able to identify a quite distinct anomaly. The contrast between the confidence that my respondents had in being able to express their individuality through their consumer goods, and the perception on their part that other teenage consumers conformed to each other, particularly in terms of fashion, was striking. On a more mundane note, perhaps the most important factor to remember in this context is the financial one.

> *Interviewer*: Does this list [of consumer goods that Paul would like to buy] reflect you as a person in any way?
> *Paul*: Yeah. It reflects I'm skint.

Consumer lifestyles are significant not only because of the opportunities they provide, but because the structural influences I discussed in Chapter 3 can have an equally important role in actively preventing access to such lifestyles. At this point, I will quote one more exchange from my group interviews. The main line of argument here is that there is significant evidence to suggest that though my respondents were fully aware of the pressures to conform that exist in consumer culture, and though they felt that these pressures had a derogatory effect on their peers, such pressures were seen at a personal level to promote the very individuality that they otherwise stifle.

Interviewer: Shannon, you said it's important for people to have certain consumer goods. In what ways do you think these are important to people?

Shannon: It's important to fit in with everybody. To fit in more *and* show what you are really like . . .

Darren: You are influenced but I don't think anybody'd buy anything just because their mates wanted something like that.

Louise: Oh no, I wouldn't.

Tony: But if you lived on a desert island with nobody else there except a few black natives or something, you wouldn't walk around in Naf Naf coats all the time . . . You'd wear a pair of jeans and a t-shirt.

Discussion

To summarize, the evidence seems to suggest that teenage consumers do indeed live on a desert island, but evidently not the island that this respondent describes. Rather, an island of consumer lifestyles where they appear to be able to buy whatever consumer goods they choose, according to their own personal tastes – which are limited only by the extent of the personal resources at their disposal. Here they can be exactly who and what they please, while only the natives are subject to the communal conformities of consumer culture. On this island, young people can feel safe from the ravages of the cruel seas (of rapid social change and inequality) that surround them. They can feel free of the risks that underlie what it means to live on a desert island. They cannot, however, escape from that island, nor from the tentacles of consumerism. And it is in this sense that consumption fails to provide young people with the service that they demand of it. The risks inherent in social pressures to consume in appropriate ways appear to be as severe as the very risks that young consumers are endeavouring to offset. Consumer lifestyles cannot provide a genuine escape from the ravages of individualization.

As far as the construction of lifestyles is concerned, consumption clearly plays an important role in young people's lives, especially in so far as such lifestyles appear to provide a resource according to which young people can relate aspects of structure and agency. If we accept Reimer's (1995: 124) definition of lifestyles as being 'the specific pattern of everyday activities that characterises an individual', then the implication is surely that research needs to pay more attention to the sorts of everyday patterns of lifestyle that I have discussed in this chapter, and in particular to how young people construct lifestyles in relation to their peers who play a fundamental role in ensuring the efficacy of consumer lifestyles. Ultimately, as Johansson and Miegel (1992) note, youth lifestyles are both conformist and creative. Unravelling this paradox should be central to any future development of a sociology of youth lifestyles.

The intention of this chapter was simply to provide a flavour of the ways in which young people interact with consumer lifestyles from day to day. I should therefore reiterate my point that consumer lifestyles are not free-standing; they represent a mirror, or at least a reaction to and interaction with the sorts of structural influences that affect young people in an ever-changing world. All sorts of other issues including class, race and gender may have a more fundamental role in constructing who it is young people actually are in the long term. But consumer lifestyles provide young people with a means of coping with the ups and downs of social change, as that change is expressed through their everyday lives. In order to illustrate this point, in the concluding chapter I want to focus on two further and related issues: the ideological influence of consumer lifestyles and the impact such lifestyles have on the construction of young people's identities at the beginning of the twenty-first century.

9
YOUTH IDENTITIES
IN A CHANGING WORLD

During the course of this book I have discussed a wide variety of influences on young people's lives. I have also suggested that the notion of youth lifestyles has the potential to provide a new dimension to, or angle on, the sociology of youth. Until now, however, I have not discussed in any real depth an equally significant proposition, namely that just as youth lifestyles cannot be experienced independently from structural constraints on young people's lives, neither can youth lifestyles be discussed without reference to the construction of youth identities. Although the ups and downs of social change are experienced through youth lifestyles, the way in which young people engage with these lifestyles is through the construction of their identities and the negotiation of the relationship between structure and agency. I want to focus on the role of identity in the context of young people's lifestyles as a means of bringing some of the threads of my overall debate to a final conclusion, or at least as a means of stimulating wider debate within the sociology of youth.

It has already been suggested that notions of youth (where youth is more of a label than an easily identifiable group or set of experiences) should not attempt to pigeon-hole young people, least of all according to their age. In other words, young people do not go through easily identifiable rites of passage. This proposition has recently been discussed in some depth by Jeffs and Smith (1998) who point out that because of male dominance in the public domain and the perceived threat young men are seen to have in respect of the dominant order, the notion of youth has acquired predominantly masculine connotations. In many respects then, and not least in the context of gender, discussions of youth tend to be rather static and often inconsequential, a state of affairs that raises some serious concerns for the future of a sociology of youth:

> This field of study has produced little of substance, and certainly almost nothing fresh or original for nearly two decades. It has become more inward looking. As a sub-discipline it is unlikely to disappear (although perhaps it should) as too many have invested too much in it. It will linger on – not least because governments continue to be concerned about 'troublesome youth' and require people to research into the topic. Despite regular injections of research funding it is likely to become increasingly irrelevant. Exhausted, reduced to picking over the minutiae of young people's lives and re-working its own tired models it will stagger on . . . As people seek out difference rather than acknowledging commonality, youth as a meaningful concept continues to slip from view.
>
> (Jeffs and Smith 1998: 59)

Much of the problem here seems to stem from the fact that youth researchers have tended to look for an assumed generational response to the patterns they describe, and as a consequence they have fallen into the trap of under-estimating the complex nature of the 'youth' experience. All sorts of class, race and gender differences are interacting in the construction of young people's lives at the turn of the century, to the extent that many young people fail to reach the holy grail of adulthood. From this point of view, 'youth' appears to represent a state of limbo within which adult statuses often seem a considerable way off. The threat of unemployment in particular casts a shadow over young people's lives, but equally over the actual funding of research into young people. Sadly, the denigration of young people and the concomitant exaggeration of the threat they pose to society as a whole attracts funding; this, in turn, creates a situation in which researchers are simply not prepared to take any real risks by way of innovative research design (see Jeffs and Smith 1998: 63). Jeffs and Smith argue that the key to a progressive understanding of young people lies in a broader conception of the totality of their experience and aspirations that does not depend on a rigid conception of age.

Although Jeffs and Smith present an insightful and, in some ways, brave analysis of the current state of the sociology of youth, I would argue that the undoubted fact that the sub-discipline has indeed ploughed the same path for so long has led them to a hasty dismissal of any notions of the age-specificity of youth. Young people do appear to be experiencing a very formative period in their lives during which they may be making crucial decisions about their futures, both in terms of their careers and their identities. Young people experience a common status in the sense that they are not yet adults and perhaps more significantly, they are very often not treated as adults by adults. The notion of identity is particularly important in any discussion of young people in that while I have argued elsewhere that consumer lifestyles appear to represent a bridge between a young person's experience of society and their experience of themselves, it is their identity that is constructed in this context. The problem appears to be then that although the sociology of youth has certainly aged considerably, it has not necessarily matured. In this respect, while a call for the premature death of the sociology of youth would be hasty, what is needed is a wholesale re-evaluation of the ideas, methodologies and concerns that underlie it. The ideological contexts in which young people construct consumer lifestyles represents one area which needs immediate attention.

Ideological aspects of consumer lifestyles

Before I come to any conclusions about the relationship between consumer lifestyles and identity, I want to clarify further the significance of the relationship between consumer lifestyles and ideology in young people's lives. I do not want to create the impression here that consumer lifestyles are the be all and end all of young people's lives as we move into the twenty-first century. However, I am calling on sociologists of youth to consider more seriously the possibility that consumption represents *the* main arena within which young people play out the relationship with structure and agency, while negotiating their role and position in an ever-changing world. Regardless of the creative nature of the meanings young people invest in their consumer lifestyles, the suggestion here is that social change has created a particular form of consciousness among young people which legitimizes conceptions of consumer culture. Young people may get as much as they want out of what they consume, but by its very nature such consumption will inevitably buttress the status quo.

Consumer lifestyles clearly have a significant ideological element. Consumer capitalism thrives by suggesting that consumers can endow meaning in consumer goods completely freely. This cannot be possible in a world where advertising and marketing are such powerful institutional influences, apparently impinging on a wide variety of aspects of everyday life. Ideologically, consumption operates at both an immediate and a very subtle level. By consuming a pair of training shoes, for example, a young person not only buys comfort and a communal sense of well-being, but also legitimizes a way of life. By consuming a pair of training shoes the individual asserts his or her rights as a citizen of consumer culture, and effectively accepts the status quo (see Urry 1990). It could, indeed, be argued in this context that nowadays the status quo is all that is on offer to the individual, partly because the individual cost of denying any sort of role for consumption in everyday settings is potentially too risky on a psycho-social level. A young person can only be accepted as an individual within the cultural contexts laid down for him or her, bearing in mind the limitations laid down on those contexts by broader structural inputs. It is almost as if an individual can offset the risks of everyday life by consuming, as my sample suggests, in similar ways to their peers; the only alternative is to face those risks head on.

Consumer capitalism claims to offer chameleon-like qualities to the consumer. It claims to be able to offer the young consumer a real sense of identity through an apparently perpetually diverse array of goods. It claims to be able to reinvent itself in order to offer a diversity of goods that can be moulded by the individual to fit his or her individual profile. However, consumer capitalism and the goods it offers in this equation are far from chameleon-like. Herein lies a great irony. Consumer capitalism is still dependent upon mass production and mass consumption which only *appear* emancipatory under the guise of individualized consumption; hence the example of 'retro' training shoes. Individuals are able to feel that they consume individually by purchasing a particular colour of training shoe, when all around them are, in fact, wearing the same shoe, but in slightly different shades. They are consuming what is essentially a mass-produced product. However reassuringly stable, and yet individualistic, purchasing a pair of 'retro' training shoes might be, underpinned by the profit motive, such trainers appear to harbour an ideological dimension of which the young consumer is arguably blissfully uncritical, and perhaps even, unaware. Ultimately, however, it is the appearance of such passivity that is, in itself, illusory, inasmuch as young consumers are fully aware of this ideological dimension. It is just that such awareness is only expressed in their role as a third party commenting upon their peers' consumption patterns. Young people do appear to be aware, at least to an extent, of the ways in which the ideology of consumerism is expressed through their lifestyles. But they are prepared, subconsciously, to give up a certain degree of individuality in exchange for the personal security this provides. However much these young people appear to be controlled, within that framework of control they are able to construct their own realities, and in this sense are in fact *in control* themselves. Regardless of the structural influences upon young people's lives, as sociologists we need to consider consumers' interpretations of such structures and not some perceived absolute truth of what constitutes and structures these lives.

I want to address the above arguments in the context of the debate surrounding post-modernity which I discussed earlier in Chapter 4. Hawkes (1996) argues that there might be an argument for describing post-modernism as the ideology of consumer capitalism. In this sense, Hawkes' discussion of the work of Zizek (1989) is useful. Zizek, reinforcing what I have suggested above, argues that ideology is not something that merely affects our ideas but happens to the totality of our existence. Ideology is common sense:

> ideology is not simply a 'false consciousness', an illusory representation of reality, it is rather this reality itself which is already to be conceived as 'ideological' . . . 'Ideological' is not the 'false consciousness' of a social being but this being in so far as it is supported by 'false consciousness'.
>
> (p. 21)

The ideology of consumerism is therefore reproduced in the commonsense form of young people's lifestyles. Zizek argues that there is nothing illusory about ideology, which he sees as accurately responding to reality. As far as Zizek is concerned, post-modern theory amounts to the ideology of consumer capitalism. Although he agrees with the post-modern contention that metaphors of depth are untenable, he argues that the finance-based economy is equally depthless in this sense, causing dire consequences for the individual. Indeed, he goes as far as to claim that the commodity economy destroys the subject. But the problem here is that post-modern theorists tend not to apply the so-called death of the subject directly to commodification, and therefore appear enthusiastically to endorse such a turn of events. 'Far from containing any kind of subversive potentials, the dispersed, plural, constructed subjects hailed by post-modern theory (the subject prone to particular, inconsistent modes of enjoyment, etc.) simply designates the form of subjectivity that corresponds to late capitalism' (Zizek 1989: 216).

Ideology, then, has become materialized, most visibly perhaps in young people's lifestyles, and as such, Zizek believes that we are living a lie which, because we live it, becomes real (Hawkes 1996). This relates to what Thomas and Thomas (1928) say about reality amounting to what the individual *perceives* to be reality, and in turn to what Dittmar (1992) refers to as the materialism-idealism paradox. This is the commonly accepted idea that every individual has a unique personality independent of material circumstances, alongside the paradoxical notion that material possessions are central regulators, not only of large-scale social processes, but also of interpersonal relations and impressions. In a so-called post-modern world, an individual may lose his or her subjectivity amid a plethora of lifestyle choices, and yet the society in which he or she lives puts considerable emphasis on the uniqueness of each and every person. This contradiction underlies young people's everyday experience of rapid social change.

As an ideology, consumerism has, in a historical sense, increasingly come to affect mundane and everyday aspects of young people's lives and young people will subsequently and inevitably reproduce dominant power structures, while often, as a result, feeling a sense of social exclusion. After all, 'the commercial links are inescapable and trenchant. All symbolic materials are supplied under determinant conditions – not from the voice of God' (Willis 1990: 130). At one level this means that young people at the start of the twenty-first century are more about continuity than they are about change. Rebellion has given way to conformity to the extent that youth cultures no longer appear to stand for the same principles as they did in the past.

But the more important point here is that regardless of the above power dimension, at the everyday level ideology is a negotiated ideology, and it is the way in which such ideologies are negotiated in everyday commonsensical settings that is of sociological interest. Ultimately, the personal factor, as Swingewood (1991) notes, is a constitutive factor of every social occurrence: 'social science cannot remain on the surface . . . but must reach the actual human experiences and attitudes which constitute the full, live and actual reality beneath the formal organisation of social institutions' (Thomas and Znaniecki 1927: 1834).

Identities and lifestyles

As far as it is possible to make conclusions about the relationship between consumer lifestyles and identity among young people, I am arguing that this relationship is a social and cultural construction. Social life amounts to a web of meanings which can be described as reality definitions (see Cashmore and Mullan 1983). Young people use consumption as a means of defining their realities. Young people, in effect, define their own reality, and if consumer lifestyles are defined as significant within that reality, then so be it.

Identities are influenced by all sorts of factors, including race, gender, family upbringing and so on. Consumer lifestyles may not have as much long-term significance as any of these factors, but for some young people it plays an invaluable role in maintaining a stable sense of coherence with which these other factors can interact. Identities are fluid, and consumption helps to ensure that such fluidity is manageable. For instance, it became clear during the research project which I discussed in Chapter 8, that there were particular codes of consumption that related to membership of an ethnic group. The street style of black working-class youths amounted to a powerful source of cultural capital which, in itself, had a significant role to play in constructing how many of those entering the shop, black or white, actually felt about themselves. Gender also came across clearly as a significant means of constructing young people's identities, and consumer goods were there to be used in a fashion that was appropriate in reasserting such identities. To reiterate, consumption is a valuable tool or resource in asserting *aspects* of young people's identities.

Having identified the ideological role of consumer lifestyles, a key question still remains: what part do consumer lifestyles play in the construction of young people's identities and how does this relate them to broader processes of social change? If perhaps one author, above all others, has managed to adequately comprehend the complexities of youth identities while relating them to the intricacies of social change and lifestyles, it is likely to be Alberto Melucci. Melucci (1992) points out that nowadays it is more difficult than ever before to actually answer the question, 'Who am I?' In this respect the gulf between the construction of traditional identities and contemporary identities is absolutely enormous. The accelerated pace of change is such that people have fewer reference points by which they can plot their life-courses, and in this respect are apparently obliged to actualize themselves as consumers in isolation. From a longer-term historical perspective, Melucci therefore discusses a situation within which young people have been transformed into social beings. A child growing up in a traditional society would have been told who they were by their elders until, at a certain stage in life, just being told was no longer enough. However much traditional society may have tried to convince them, the individuals concerned simply could not accept what their culture told them they were. That had to be interpreted at an individual level. However, communal tests or 'rites of passage' were still constructed in order that the transition into adulthood or the construction of identity could be confirmed along social parameters. But, as Melucci points out, such initiation rights are not as enforceable, nor indeed as prevalent, in contemporary society which is far less stable and within which identities are far more likely to be achieved, as opposed to ascribed.

In this context, Melucci argues that what distinguishes society is its multiplication of memberships. An individual is not defined by his or her relationship to a specific place or trade, but according to a multiplicity of memberships:

> We participate simultaneously in a number of areas, groups, and dimensions of social and cultural life; we are consumers, we use services, we participate to varying extents in social and cultural life, we are members of associations, parties, groups and clans of various kinds. In each of these settings we live a part of ourselves, certain dimensions of our personalities and experience. We are therefore no longer defined by a single identification criterion, such as being born into a particular family or pursuing a certain trade. This has given rise to a proliferation of the ways in which individuals define themselves . . . It is less easy for individuals to forecast their progress through life and none of us can confidently predict everything that will mark our futures; futures so much more open to a range of possible and unforeseeable factors than ever before in the past.
>
> (Melucci 1992: 54)

The suggestion here would be that although we all experience this process, young people are more exposed to what Melucci calls a 'pluralization of life opportunities' than any other social group. Again, the process of globalization is especially influential here in so far as it expands the stimuli and opportunities open to young people. The key point is that people's material conditions do not simply map out their identities, but those identities are increasingly constructed through symbolic sources. Hence the key role of young people's lifestyles. Young people, as Melucci points out, are especially receptive to imagery and a flow of messages is simultaneously focused directly at them, largely via the global media.

Melucci's attempt to discuss the peculiar nature of young people's identity constructions become increasingly pertinent to the themes of this book. He points out that the transition between youth and adulthood is far less clear cut than it ever has been in the past. In this sense youth is far more of a cultural process than it is a biological one: 'People are not young, because, or only because, they have a certain age, but because they follow certain styles of consumption, or certain codes of behaviour and dress' (p. 56). For this reason adolescence is inevitably prolonged and the question of identity becomes less easy to answer. In other words, social change is such that it becomes increasingly difficult for the individual to judge who he or she is or what he or she is becoming.

The problem with the above scenario according to Melucci is the fact that the vast range of symbolic possibilities open to young people do not actually provide the appropriate conditions within which they can adequately test their identities. The traditional sources of identity associated with the family, for instance, have not been replaced with a convincing alternative. Consumer lifestyles play a potentially significant role in the construction of young people's identities, but their impact may not be wholly positive. In this context, Melucci goes out of his way to point out that he is not

> here to preach against consumerism. Consumer society is complex and ambivalent; to consume is to express choice, preference, need, desire, and does not just mean manipulation by the media. I believe, however, that the indiscriminate possibility to consume fosters the loss of a decisive human experience – the requirement of limitation. We are individuals because we exist as entities that differ from others, because we recognize ourselves as limited. As the well-known dictum runs: *Omnis determinato est negatio*.
>
> (p. 57)

Melucci's argument then is that consumerism provides young people with an environment within which they feel anything is possible. For instance, young people can consume designer drugs and by doing so fulfil some form of a need, but quite possibly at considerable cost. According to Melucci, although heroin, for example, will probably turn into a concrete risk, a young person might take it, as a fake challenge which does nothing to address the essential weakness of the personality, thereby perpetuating the constant state of indeterminacy that the young person appears to find themselves in. Consumer lifestyles therefore arguably make young people and consumers in general feel omnipotent, when what they are really doing is blinding themselves to the uncertain realities of real life.

Melucci's discussion raises all sorts of questions not only about the nature of youth identities, but also about how young people interact with broad social change. He appears to illustrate how effective young people are as barometers of social change, but also highlights the need to look closely at how that change is manifested in the actualities of young people's everyday lives. The suggestion here is that despite the problems Melucci outlines, we live in a society in which young people are becoming increasingly agentic, 'Adolescents are not simply containers to be filled by values and moral rules, but rather they are increasingly agents of their own development and they experience all the contradictions of such a challenge' (Melucci 1992: 59).

A key factor as far as Melucci is concerned then is that young people are in the position to frame their own reality through 'cognitive, cultural and material investments' (p. 60). Youth is therefore an increasingly nomadic experience as the individual attempts to come to terms with the excessive possibilities provided for them by a fragmenting culture. Young people's identities are less something they 'have' and more something they 'do'. The problem for young people is that the promise of a so-called 'post-modern' culture cannot always be fulfilled. The abundance that culture seems to provide can encourage a feeling of emptiness, repetition and isolation. The degree of fragmentation characterizing contemporary culture is such that the individual is having constantly to change form, cherishing the unique temporality of the present. From this perspective young people are perceptive receptor's of today's culture and the dilemmas of time it presents to people on an everyday basis: 'By paying the price of personal and collective suffering, they remind us that the time of too many possibilities can be a possibility without time, without limits, without choices' (Melucci 1992: 65).

It would be misleading to imply that Melucci's position has gone unchallenged. Many commentators adopting a more traditional approach to youth continue to insist that although significant, consumer lifestyles do not play any fundamental role in the construction of people's identities. Ken Roberts (1997), for example, argues that leisure and consumer lifestyles are simply not equipped to support young people's identity constructions and that traditional social divisions play a far more significant role in determining who and what it is young people are. Roberts therefore notes that there have been some significant changes in the nature of youth cultures: the movement of more and more young women away from the privacy of their bedrooms and into the public arena is particularly significant in this respect. The rise of 'girl power' has arguably contributed to a situation in which growing optimism among young women about their futures appears to be allied to a growing pessimism among boys. This creates a whole new spin on the nature of gender relationships in a changing world (Arlidge 1999). Consumer culture may be playing a more active role in providing subject positions for young women (McRobbie 1993). More broadly, a concomitant trend towards individualization and the emergence of a pick 'n' mix culture may represent valid aspects of social change but such change will still only have a partial impact on who it is young people are:

> Leisure can make people satisfied with whatever they are but it does not tell them who they basically are . . . Lifestyle experimentation can appear attractive. Yet people are liable to find their lifestyles, and the social positions and identities that they thereby create for themselves, disintegrating almost as quickly as they are constructed.
> (Roberts 1997: 11)

From Roberts's point of view then, regardless of the degree of social change young people's lifestyles are still largely about having fun. Lifestyles, in effect, are still constructed *within* social classes. Factors such as sex, sexuality, social class and in some cases, nationality, religion and ethnicity are still the fundamental determinants of identity, even if they are often more ambiguous than they were in the past. As far as Roberts is concerned, leisure is basically just about play and pleasure and does not have any more significance or meaning than that. It is at this juncture that I have to disagree. His argument that leisure and lifestyles are not equipped to support identity formation is a valid one, but he does not take this argument far enough. Just because lifestyles do not provide the stable sorts of identities other forms of social support may have done in the past does not mean to say that they do not represent a fundamental influence on identity construction. Social change is such that the very nature and indeed role of identity has changed and young people have changed with it.

The point here is that young people's identities are increasingly unstable and that in a rapidly changing world the traditional forms of support Roberts discusses are simply no longer appropriate. Young people do call upon their lifestyles to construct who it is they are precisely because such lifestyles provide them with the flexibility they need. Roberts (1997) is correct in the sense that lifestyles are not equipped to provide young people with stability, but that is not a role young people want their lifestyle to play. The fact that lifestyles are unstable actively helps them to cope with the instabilities and uncertainties of social change. If young people's identities are unstable as a consequence then so be it. This is a point most graphically expressed in the work of Zygmunt Bauman:

> And so the snag is no longer how to discover, invent, construct assemble (even buy) an identity, but how to prevent it from

sticking. Well constructed and durable identity turns from an asset into a liability. The hub of postmodern life strategy is not identity building, but avoidance of fixation.

(Bauman 1996: 24)

This book has argued that young people are having to deal with the dilemmas of rapid social, cultural and structural change as a routine part of their everyday lives and that a primary means by which they deal with this situation is through the maintenance of consumer lifestyles. Consumer lifestyles effectively provide a vehicle or a currency through which fluid identities are constructed. A consumer imperative has therefore emerged as a fundamental means of stabilizing young people's lives at the turn of the century. Such stability is not manifested in the form of a deep-rooted sense of sameness, but in a flexible, mutable and diverse sense of identity within which consumerism appears to present the only viable resource:

Rather than unreflexively adopting a lifestyle, through tradition or habit, the new heroes of consumer culture make lifestyle a life project and display their individuality and sense of style in the particularity of the assemblage of goods, clothes, practices, experiences, appearance and bodily dispositions they design together in a lifestyle.

(Featherstone 1987: 59)

Concluding discussion

I argued in Chapter 1 that the development of the sociology of youth has been hindered by a tendency to concentrate on melodramatic expressions of, or structurally loaded discussions of 'problematic' youth which have limited relevance to young people's lives in general. The intention of my discussion of consumer lifestyles and ideologies was to illustrate how young people's lives at the start of the twenty-first century are potentially more about continuity than they are about change. This may seem paradoxical in light of what I have just said about the changing nature of identity and thus needs further explanation. Young people's lifestyles appear to play a dual role. Young people exploit the flexibility they can find in their lifestyles, which makes them *feel* as though their lives are stable, when what such lifestyles are actually providing is a resource for the negotiation of instability. Young people's lifestyles are therefore concerned with the *continuity of change*. But what is most important here is that young people perceive their identities to be suitable in this context. It is in this sense that, 'If men [sic] define situations as real, they are real in their consequences' (Thomas and Thomas 1928: 572).

Youth lifestyles do play an important role in young people's lives, precisely because young people actively perceive their lifestyles to be important. In this context, perhaps the key point to make in this conclusion relates back to the debate over structure and agency. As Reimer (1988) notes in his discussion of the post-materialist thesis, objective social structures *do* impose meaning on young people. However, such an imposition represents nothing more than a framework within which the same young people make sense of their own realities. Young people may not have 'real' economic power, as Jones and Martin (1999) suggest, but what power they do have they use in the active construction of their own life and their own everyday relationships. Given this, the degree of power they impart on the marketplace is virtually irrelevant. I would not for one minute dispute the contention of Bynner *et al.* (1997) that the experience of many young people is characterized by an increasing sense of anxiety, depression and even despair. But when he asks whether or not young people have the necessary human and social capital to succeed in a post-modern world, I would have to say, yes, they most certainly do, and consumer lifestyles have an important role to play in their dealing with social change in this context. Young people do not play simply for fun but to feel that they belong in a world which often appears to legislate actively against such a feeling.

To put this another way, young people use their lifestyles, which on the surface appear to be fragmented or 'post-modern', as a highly rational and modernist way of stabilizing their everyday lives. Although such lifestyles are inevitably ideologically loaded they fulfil a need for young people. They provide stability in what is essentially a largely unwelcoming world. Young people have grown up in a world in which consumerism is a way of life (see Miles 1998). The ideological power of consumerism lies in the fact that it is perceived to be natural. But consumer lifestyles are especially natural to young people who recognize the limitations of consumerism, and are prepared to put up with them in exchange for its advantages and in order to cope with the ravages of structural–cultural uncertainty. Young people use their lifestyles to navigate the structural–cultural dilemmas of social change. It is in this sense that youth lifestyles have been de-territorialized. Young people no longer depend on subcultural affirmation for the construction of their identities (if indeed they ever did) but construct lifestyles that are as adaptable and as flexible as the world around them.

To conclude, the sociology of youth faces a Herculean task if it is to adapt to the changing nature of the world around it and the young people who occupy that world. Youth, as McRobbie (1993) suggests, is not a stable undifferentiated category, and yet the sociology of youth continues to attempt to apply stable undifferentiated categories to the youth experience. For this reason, the sociology of youth has manifestly failed to come to terms with young people's relationship with rapid social change. In this respect, Williamson's (1997) point that young people's lifestyles are about living for the present is highly pertinent. The irony of social life in general is that regardless of long-term change people *feel* social change in the present. The task for the sociologist is therefore to construct reflexive focused studies of the sociological present in which the meanings that people apply to everyday contexts are actively addressed. Young people in particular are not simply products of social change but actively engage with it in complex and often apparently paradoxical ways.

Perhaps the future for the sociology of youth should be all about actively engaging with a world that is just as much about continuity – or at least young people's everyday need to maintain such continuity – as it is about the ramifications of social change. To this end I want to suggest that the best way of looking at youth, or at least of justifying the existence of a sociology of youth, is by defining it as 'the doing of specific types of work on the self' (Tait 1993: 52). The sociology of youth should therefore not be about patterns of youth experience but about how social change actively impinges on individuals' lives. Social change is such that youth is not what it used to be, and the sociology of youth should adapt to reflect this. Above all, the subdiscipline needs to address the ways in which young people actively construct their identities in individualized settings and what those constructions *mean* to the young people concerned. The threat associated with extended 'transitions' are not constant in all young people's lives, and may only affect the construction of a young person's identity on a temporary basis. Youth lifestyles on the other hand, serve to orientate young people to the ups and downs of everyday life. In that respect, they provide continuity in an ever-changing world. Ultimately, young people are young not because of their age but because of what they do and how and why they do it. For this reason alone, the time has come for the sociologist of youth to pay considerably more attention to the everyday construction of youth lifestyles in a changing world.

Recommended reading

Jeffs, Tony and Smith, Mark (1998) The problem of 'youth' for youth work, *Youth and Policy*, 62: 45–66.
Includes a critical thought-provoking analysis of the current state of the sociology of youth.
Melucci, Antonio (1992) Youth silence and voice: selfhood and commitment in the everyday experience of adolescents, in J. Fornäs and G. Bolin (eds) *Moves in Modernity*. Stockholm: Almqvist and Wiksell International, pp. 51–71.
A stimulating piece that actively attempts to come to terms with the changing nature of young people's identities in an ever-changing world.

REFERENCES

Abercrombie, N. (1994) Authority and consumer society, in R. Keat, N. Whiteley and N. Abercrombie (eds) *The Authority of the Consumer*. London: Routledge, pp. 43–57.

Abrams, M. (1959) *The Teenage Consumer*. London: Press Exchange.

Adamski, W. and Grootings, P. (eds) (1989) *Youth, Education and Work in Europe*. London: Routledge.

Adorno, T. (1990) On popular music, in S. Frith and A. Goodwin (eds) *On Record: Rock, Pop and the Written Word*. London: Routledge, pp. 301–14.

Albrow, M. (1997) The impact of globalization on sociological concepts: community, culture and milieu, in J. Eade (ed.) *Living the Global City: Globalization as Local Process*. London: Routledge, pp. 20–36.

Aldridge, J. W. (1969) *In the Country of the Young*. New York: Harper's Magazine Press.

Allen, J. and Massey, D. (eds) (1995) *Geographical Worlds*. Oxford: Oxford University Press.

Alloway, N. and Gilbert, P. (1998) Video game culture: playing with masculinity, violence and pleasure, in S. Howard (ed.) *Wired-Up: Young People and the Electronic Media*. London: UCL Press, pp. 95–115.

Appleyard, B. (1995) 'Time we all learnt to grow up', *Independent*, 31 May.

Archer, M. (1995) *Realist Social Theory: The Morphogenetic Approach*. Cambridge: Cambridge University Press.

Arlidge, J. (1999) Girl power gives boys a crisis of confidence, *Observer*, 14 March, p. 3.

Auderheide, P. (1986) The look of the sound, in T. Gitlin (ed.) *Watching Television*. New York: Pantheon, pp. 11–135.

Barker, R. (1997) *Political Ideas in Modern Britain*, 2nd edn. London: Routledge.

Baudrillard, J. (1983) *Simulations*. New York: Semiotext(e).

Baudrillard, J. (1988) Consumer society, in M. Poster (ed.) *Selected Writings*. Cambridge: Polity Press.

Bauman, Z. (1996) From pilgrim to tourist – or a short history of identity, in S. Hall and P. Du Gay (eds) *Questions of Cultural Identity*. London: Sage.

Bauman, Z. (1998) *Globalization: The Human Consequences*. Cambridge: Polity Press.

Beck, U. (1992) *Risk Society: Towards a New Modernity*. London: Sage.

Bellah, R., Madson, R., Sullivan, W. M., Swidler, A. and Tipton, S. M. (1985) *Habits of the Heart: Middle America Observed*. London: Hutchinson.

Best, S. and Kellner, D. (1998) Beavis and Butt-Head: no future for postmodern youth, in J. S. Epstein (ed.) *Youth Culture: Identity in a Postmodern World*. Oxford: Blackwell, pp. 74–99.

Bhaba, H. (1990) *Narrating the Nation*. London: Routledge.

Billington, R., Hockey, J. and Strawbridge, S. (1998) *Exploring Self and Society*. Basingstoke: Macmillan.

Blaikie, N. (1993) *Approaches to Social Enquiry*. Cambridge: Polity Press.

Bocock, R. (1993) *Consumption*. London: Routledge.

Boëthius, U. (1995) Controlled pleasures: youth and literary texts, in J. Förnas and G. Bolin, *Youth Culture and Late Modernity*. London: Sage, pp. 145–68.

Bourdieu, P. (1984) *Distinction: A Social Critique of the Judgement of Taste*. London: Routledge and Kegan Paul.

Branson, J. and Miller, D. (1991) Pierre Bourdieu, in P. Beilharz (ed.) *Social Theory: A Guide to Central Thinkers*. Sydney: Allen and Unwin, pp. 37–45.

Brinkley, I. (1997) Underworked and underpaid, *Soundings*, 6: 161–71.

Bryant, C. and Jary, D. (1991) *Giddens' Theory of Structuration*. London: Routledge.

Buckingham, D. (ed.) (1993) *Reading Audiences: Young People and the Media*. Manchester: Manchester University Press.

Buckingham, D. (1997) Electronic child abuse? Rethinking the media's effects on children, in M. Parker and J. Petley, *Ill Effects: The Media/Violence Debate*. London: Routledge, pp. 32–47.

Bynner, J. E., Ferri, E. and Shepherd, P. (1997) *Twenty-Something in the 1990s: Getting On, Getting By, Getting Nowhere*. Aldershot: Ashgate.

Calcutt, A. (1998) *Arrested Development: Popular Culture and the Erosion of Adulthood*. London: Cassell.

Campbell, C. (1987) *The Romantic Ethic and the Spirit of Modern Consumerism*. Oxford: Blackwell.

Cashmore, E. E. (1984) *No Future: Youth and Society*. London: Heinemann.

Cashmore, E. E. and Mullan, B. (1983) *Approaching Social Theory*. London: Heinemann.

Chaney, D. (1996) *Lifestyles*. London: Routledge.

Cohen, P. (1997) *Rethinking the Youth Question: Education, Labour and Cultural Studies*. London: Macmillan.

Cohen, S. (1980) *Folk Devils and Moral Panics: The Creation of the Mods and Rockers*. Oxford: Blackwell.

Coles, B. (1995) *Youth and Social Policy: Youth Citizenship and Young Careers*. London: UCL Press.

Côté, J. and Allahar, A. L. (1996) *Generation on Hold: Coming of Age in the Late Twentieth Century*. London: New York University Press.

Craik, J. (1994) *The Face of Fashion: Cultural Studies in Fashion*. London: Routledge.

Davis, J. (1990) *Youth and the Condition of Britain*. London: Athlone.

DeCerteau, M. (1984) *The Practice of Everyday Life*. Berkeley: University of California Press.

Department of Education and Science survey (1983) *Young People in the 80's: A Survey*. London: HMSO.

Dittmar, H. (1992) *The Social Psychology of Material Possessions: To Have Is to Be*. Hemel Hempstead: Harvester Wheatsheaf.

Douglas, M. (1992) *Risk and Blame: Essays in Cultural Theory*. London: Routledge.

Drotner, K. (1991) *At skabe sig – selv*. Ungdom, æsteik, pædagogik, Københaven: Glydendsal, pp. 145–68.

Drotner, K. (1992) Modernity and media panics, in M. Skovmand and K. Schröder (eds) *Media Cultures: Reappraising Transnational Media*. London: Routledge.

Dubow, E. and Miller, L. (1996) Television violence viewing and aggressive behavior, in T. MacBeth (ed.) *Tuning in to Young Viewers: Social Science Perspectives on Television*. London: Sage, pp. 117–47.

Ehrenreich, B., Hess, E. and Jacobs, G. (1997) Beatlemania: a sexually deviant consumer culture?, in K. Gelder and K. Thornton, *The Subcultures Reader*. London: Routledge, pp. 523–36.

Epstein, J. S. (ed.) (1998) *Youth Culture: Identity in a Postmodern World*. Oxford: Blackwell.

Evans, E., Rutberg, J. and Sather, C. (1991) Content analysis of contemporary teen magazines for adolescent females, *Youth and Society*, 23: 99–120.

Ewen, S. and Ewen, E. (1982) *Channels of Desire*. New York: McGraw-Hill.

Featherstone, M. (1987) Lifestyle and consumer culture, *Theory, Culture and Society*, 4: 55–70.

Featherstone, M. (1991) *Consumer Culture and Postmodernism*. London: Sage.

Fisher, S. and Holder, S. (1981) *Too Much Too Young?* London: Pan.

Fornäs, J. and Bolin, G. (1992) *Moves in Modernity*. Stockholm: Almqvist and Wiksell International.

Fowler, D. (1995) *The First Teenagers: The Lifestyle of Young Wage Earners in Interwar Britain*. London: Woburn Press.

Friedman, J. (1990) Being in the world: globalization and localization, *Theory, Culture and Society*, 7(2–3): 311–28.

Frith, S. (1978) *The Sociology of Rock*. London: Constable.

Furedi, F. (1997) *The Culture of Fear: Risk-Taking and the Morality of Low Expectation*. London: Cassell.

Furlong, A. and Cartmel, F. (1997) *Young People and Social Change*. Buckingham: Open University Press.

Gaines, D. (1991) *Teenage Wasteland: Suburbia's Dead End Kids*. New York: Pantheon.

Gelder, K. and Thornton, S. (eds) (1997) *The Subcultures Reader*. London: Routledge.

Giddens, A. (1976) *New Rules of Sociological Method*. London: Hutchinson.

Giddens, A. (1984) *The Constitution of Society: Outline of the Theory of Structuration*. Cambridge: Polity Press.

Giddens, A. (1991) *Modernity and Self-Identity: Self and Society in the Late Modern Age*. Cambridge: Polity Press.

Gillespie, M. (1995) *Television, Ethnicity and Cultural Change*. London: Routledge.

Giroux, H. (1994) *Disturbing Pleasures*. New York: Routledge.

Green, B., Reid, J.-A. and Bigum, C. (1998) Teaching the Nintendo generation? Children, computer culture and popular technologies, in S. Howard (ed.) (1998) *Wired-Up: Young People and the Electronic Media*. London: UCL Press, pp. 19–41.

Green, J. (1997) *Risk and Misfortune: The Social Construction of Accidents*. London: UCL Press.

Griffin, C. (1993) *Representations of Youth: The Study of Youth and Adolescence in Britain and America*. Cambridge: Polity Press.

Griffin, C. (1997) Troubled teens: Managing disorders of transition and consumption, *Feminist Review*, 55: 4–21, Spring.

Gunter, B. and Furnham, A. (1998) *Children as Consumers: A Psychological Analysis of the Young People's Market*. London: Routledge.

Hannerz, U. (1992) *Cultural Complexity: Studies in the Social Organization of Meaning*. New York: Colombia University Press.

Harris, D. (1997) *Society of Signs*. London: Routledge.

Harvey, D. (1989) *The Condition of Postmodernity*. Oxford: Blackwell.

Hawkes, D. (1996) *Ideology*. London: Routledge.

Hebdige, D. (1979) *Subculture: The Meaning of Style*. New York: Methuen.

Hendry, L. B., Shucksmith, J., Love, J. G. and Glendinning, A. (1993) *Young People's Leisure and Lifestyles*. London: Routledge.

Hollands, R. (1995) *Friday Night, Saturday Night*. Newcastle: Newcastle University Press.

Horkheimer, M. and Adorno, T. (1973) *Dialectic of Enlightenment*. London: Allen Lane.

Huq, R. (1997). Paradigm lost? youth and pop in the 90s, *Soundings*, 6: 180–7, Summer.

Irwin, S. (1995) Social reproduction and change in the transition from youth to adulthood, *Sociology*, May, 29(2): 293–316.

Jameson, F. (1984) Postmodernism, or the cultural logic of late capitalism, *New Left Review*, 146: 53–93.

Jeffs, T. and Smith, M. K. (1998) The problem of 'youth' for youth work, *Youth and Policy*, 62: 45–66.

Jenkins, R. (1983) *Lads, Citizens and Ordinary Kids: Working-Class Youth Lifestyles in Belfast*. London: Routledge and Kegan Paul.

Jessor, R., Donnovan, J. E. and Costa, F. M. (1990) *Beyond Adolescence*. Cambridge: Cambridge University Press.

Johansson, T. and Miegel, F. (1992) *Do the Right Thing: Lifestyle and Identity in Contemporary Youth Culture*. Malmo: Graphic Systems.

Johnsson-Smaragdi, U. (1994) Models of change and stability in adolescents; media use, in K. E. Rosengren (ed.) *Media Effects and Beyond: Culture, Socialization and Lifestyles*. London: Routledge, pp. 97–130.

Jones, G. (1995) *Leaving Home*. Buckingham: Open University Press.

Jones, G. and Martin, C. (1997) *The Social Context of Spending in Youth*. Centre for Educational Sociology Briefing, University of Edinburgh, no. 11, June.

Jones, G. and Martin, C. (1999) The 'young consumer' at home: dependence, resistance and autonomy, in J. Hearn and S. Roseneil (eds) *Consuming Cultures: Power and Resistance*. Basingstoke: Macmillan, pp. 17–41.

Jones, G. and Wallace, C. (1992) *Youth, Family and Citizenship*. Buckingham: Open University Press.

Keane, J. (1997) Ecstasy in the unhappy society, *Soundings*, 6: 127–39, Summer.

Kelly, G. (1955) *The Psychology of Personal Constructs*. New York: Norton.

Key Note Market Review (1994) *Industry Trends and Forecasts: The Youth Market in the U.K.*, ed. P. Smith. Hampton: Keynote.

Kinder, M. (1991) *Playing With Power in Movies, Television and Video Games*. Berkeley, CA: University of California Press.

Kingdom, J. (1992) *No Such Thing as Society? Individualism and Community*. Buckingham: Open University Press.

Kubey, R. W. (1996) Television dependence, diagnosis and prevention: with commentary on video games, pornography and media education, in T. MacBeth (ed.) *Tuning in to Young Viewers: Social Science Perspectives on Television*. London: Sage, pp. 221–60.

Kumar, K. (1995) *From Post-Industrial to Post-Modern Society*. Cambridge: Blackwell.

Langman, L. (1992) Neon cages: shopping for subjectivity, in R. Shields (ed.) *Lifestyle Shopping: The Subject of Consumption*. London: Routledge, pp. 40–82.

Lash, S. (1990) *Sociology of Postmodernism*. London: Routledge.

Layder, D. (1994) *Understanding Social Theory*. London: Sage.

Leadbetter, C. (1989) 'Power to the person', in S. Hall and M. Jacques (eds) *New Times: The Changing Face of Politics in the 1990s*. London: Lawrence and Wishart, pp. 137–59.

Lee, M. L. (1993) *Consumer Culture Reborn: The Cultural Politics of Consumption*. London: Routledge.

Lopiano-Misdom, J. and De Luca, J. (1997) *Street Trends: How Today's Alternative Markets are Creating Tomorrow's Mainstream Markets*. New York: HarperCollins.

Lyon, D. (1994) *Postmodernity*. Buckingham: Open University Press.

McCabe, M. (1980) Conservative consumer typifies new generation, *Advertising Age*, pp. S–23–4.

MacDonald, R. (ed.) (1997) *Youth, the 'Underclass' and Social Exclusion*. London: Routledge.

MacDonald, R. (1998) Youth, transitions and social exclusion: some issues for youth research in the UK, *Journal of Youth Studies*, June, 1(2).

McGuigan, J. (1992) *Cultural Populism*. London: Routledge.

MacInnes, C. (1961) *England, Half English*. London: MacGibbon and Kee.

Mackay, H. (1997) *Consumption and Everyday Life*. London: Sage/Open University.

McNamee, S. (1998) Youth, gender and video games: power and control in the home, in T. Skelton and G. Valentine (eds) *Cool Places: Geographies of Youth Cultures*. London: Routledge, pp. 195–206.

McNeal, J. U. (1992) *Kids as Customers*. New York: Lexington Books.

McRobbie, A. (1993) Shut up and dance: youth culture and changing modes of femininity, *Cultural Studies*, 7: 406–26.

McRobbie, A. (1994) *Postmodernism and Popular Culture*. London: Routledge.

Maguire, M. and Maguire, S. (1997) Young people and the labour market, in R. MacDonald, *Youth, the 'Underclass' and Social Exclusion*. London: Routledge, pp. 26–38.

Malbon, B. (1998) Clubbing, consumption, identity and the spatial practices of every-night life, in T. Skelton and G. Valentine (eds) *Cool Places: Geographies of Youth Cultures*. London: Routledge, pp. 266–89.

Manning, T. (1996) Meet the E-culturati, *New Statesman and Society*, 23 February.

Marquand, D. (1996) Moralists and hedonists, in D. Marquand and A. Seldon (eds) *The Ideas That Shaped Post-War Britain*. London: Fontana, pp. 5–28.

Marquand, D. and Seldon, A. (eds) (1996) *The Ideas That Shaped Post-War Britain*. London: Fontana.

Marsland, D. (1993) *Understanding Youth: Issues and Methods in Social Education*. St Albans: Claridge.

Melechi, A. (1993) The ecstasy of disappearance, in S. Redhead (ed.), *Rave Off: Politics and Deviance in Contemporary Youth Culture*. Aldershot: Avebury.

Melucci, A. (1992) Youth silence and voice: selfhood and commitment in the everyday experience of adolescents, in J. Fornäs and G. Bolin, *Moves in Modernity*. Stockholm: Almqvist and Wiksell International, pp. 51–71.

Middleton, S., Ashworth, K. and Walker, R. (1994) *Family Fortunes: Pressures on Parents and Children in the 1990s*. London: CPAG.

Miles, S. (1996) The cultural capital of consumption: understanding 'postmodern' identities in a cultural context, *Culture & Psychology*, 2(2): 139–58.

Miles, S. (1997) ' "You just wear what you want don't yer?" An empirical examination of the relationship between youth consumption and the construction of identity', unpublished PhD thesis. University of Huddersfield.

Miles, S. (1998) *Consumerism as a Way of Life*. London: Sage.

Miles, S. and Anderson, A. (1999) 'Just do it?' Young people, the global media and the construction of consumer meanings, in A. Ralph, J. Langham and T. Lees (eds) *Youth and the Global Media*. Luton: Luton University Press, pp. 105–12.

Miles, S., Cliff, D. and Burr, V. (1997) 'Fitting in and sticking out': consumption, consumer meanings and the construction of young people's identities, *Journal of Youth Studies*, 1(1): 81–96.

Miller, D. (1987) *Material Culture and Mass Consumption*. Oxford: Basil Blackwell.

Miller, J. (1995) *Voxpop: The New Generation X Speaks*. London: Virgin.

Ministry of Education (1947) *School Life: A First Inquiry into the Transition from School to Independent Life*, Clarke Report. London: HMSO.

Mintel (1988) *Special Report: British Lifestyles*. London: Mintel.

Mitterauer, M. (1992) Youth groups in transformation, in J. Fornäs and G. Bolin, *Moves in Modernity*. Stockholm: Almqvist and Wiksell International, pp. 27–49.

Moorhouse, H. (1989) Models of work, models of leisure, in C. Rojek (ed.) *Leisure for Leisure: Critical Essays*. London: Macmillan.

Morrow, V. and Richards, M. (1996) *Transitions to Adulthood: A Family Matter?* York: York Publishing Services.

Muggleton, D. (1997) 'The subculturalist', in S. Redhead, D. Wynne and J. O'Connor, *The Club Cultures Reader*. Oxford: Blackwell, pp. 185–203.

Mungham, G. and Pearson, G. (1976) *Working Class Youth Culture*. London: Routledge and Kegan Paul.

Nava, A. and Nava, O. (1990) Discriminating or duped? *Magazine of Cultural Studies*, 5: 15–21.

Osgerby, B. (1998a) *Youth in Britain Since 1945*. Oxford: Blackwell.

Osgerby, B. (1998b) The good, the bad and the ugly: postwar media representations of youth, in A. Briggs and P. Cobley (eds) *The Media: An Introduction*. Harlow: Longman, pp. 322–34.

Palladino, G. (1996) *Teenagers: An American History*. New York: Basic Books.

Plant, M. and Plant, M. (1992) *Risk-Takers: Alcohol, Drugs, Sex and Youth*. London: Routledge.

Plummer, K. (1981) Going gay: identities, life cycles, and lifestyles in the male gay world, in J. Hart and D. Richardson (eds) *The Theory and Practice of Homosexuality*. London: Routledge.

Polhemus, T. (1994) *Streetstyle: From Sidewalk to Catwalk*. London: Thames and Hudson.

Popple, K. and Kirby, R. (1997) Winners and losers: young people in Europe, in T. Spybey (ed.) *Britain in Europe*. London: Routledge, pp. 161–72.

Presdee, M. (1990) Creating poverty and creating crime: Australian youth policy in the 1980s, in C. Wallace and M. Cross (eds) *Youth in Transition*. Basingstoke: Falmer.

Prokhorov, A., Perry, C., Kelder, S. and Klepp, K.-I. (1993) Lifestyle values of adolescents: results from Minnesota Heart Health Youth Program, *Adolescence*, 28(111), Fall.

Redhead, S. (ed.) (1993) *Rave Off: Politics and Deviance in Contemporary Youth Culture*. Aldershot: Avebury.

Redhead, S. (ed.) (1997) *Post-Fandom and the Millennial Blues*. London: Routledge.

Reimer, B. (1988) No values – new values? Youth and postmaterialism, *Scandinavian Political Studies*, 11(4): 347–59.

Reimer, B. (1995) Youth and modern lifestyles, in J. Förnas and G. Bolin (eds) *Youth Culture in Late Modernity*. London: Sage, pp. 120–44.

Reynolds, S. (1998) *Energy Flash: A Journey Through Rave Music and Dance Culture*. London: Picador.

Richard, B. and Kruger, H. (1998) Ravers' paradise? German youth cultures in the 1990s, in T. Skelton and G. Valentine (eds) *Cool Places: Geographies of Youth Cultures*. London: Routledge, pp. 161–74.

Ritzer, G. (1992) *Contemporary Sociological Theory*. London: McGraw-Hill.

Roberts, K. (1995) *Youth Employment in Modern Britain*. Oxford: Oxford University Press.

Roberts, K. (1997) Same activities, different meanings: British youth cultures in the 1990s, *Leisure Studies*, 16: 1–15.

Rojek, C. (1985) *Capitalism and Leisure Theory*. London: Tavistock.

Rojek, C. (ed.) (1989) *Leisure for Leisure: Critical Essays*. Basingstoke: Macmillan.

Rosenau, P. M. (1992) *Post-Modernism and the Social Sciences*. Princeton, NJ: Princeton University Press.

Rosengren, K. E. (1994) *Media Effects and Beyond: Culture, Socialization and Lifestyles*. London: Routledge.

Rushkoff, D. (1997) *Children of Chaos: Surviving the End of the World as We Know It*. London: Flamingo.

Rutherford, J. (1997) Introduction, *Soundings*, (6): 112–26, Summer.

Savage, J. (1997) The sound of acid, *Guardian*, 31 January.

Seabrook, J. (1978) *What Went Wrong? Working People and the Ideals of the Labour Movement*. London: Victor Gollancz.

Simmel, G. (1957) Fashion, *American Journal of Sociology*, 62: 541–8 (originally published 1904).

Simmel, G. (1978) *The Philosophy of Money*. London: Routledge and Kegan Paul (originally published 1907).

Skilbeck, M., Connell, H., Lowe, N. and Tait, K. (1994) *The Vocational Quest: New Directions in Education and Training*. London: Routledge.

Smith, R. J. and Maughan, T. (1998) Youth culture and the making of the post-Fordist economy: Dance music in contemporary Britain, *Journal of Youth Studies*, 1(2): 211–28, June.

Sobel, M. (1981) *Lifestyle and Social Structure: Concepts, Definitions, Analyses*. New York: Academic Press.

Sobel, M. (1983) Lifestyle expenditure in contemporary America: relations between stratification and culture, *American Behavioral Scientist*, 26(4): 521–33, March/April.

Solomon, M., Bamossy, G. and Askegaard, S. (1999) *Consumer Behaviour: A European Perspective*. London: Prentice Hall.

Spybey, T. (1996) *Globalization and World Society*. Cambridge: Polity Press.

Starkey, M. (1989) *Born to Shop*. Eastbourne: Monarch.

Stebbins, R. A. (1997) Lifestyle as a generic concept in ethnographic research, *Quality and Quantity*, 31: 347–60.

Steele, J. R. and Brown, J. D. (1995) Adolescent room culture: studying media in the context of everyday life, *Journal of Youth and Adolescence*, 24(5): 551–76.

Stewart, F. (1992) The adolescent as consumer, in J. C. Coleman and C. Warren-Anderson (eds) *Youth Policy in the 1990s: The Way Forward*. London: Routledge, pp. 203–26.

Stratton, J. (1985) Youth subcultures and their cultural contexts, *Australian and New Zealand Journal of Sociology*, 21: 194–218, July.

Street, J. (1997) Across the universe: the limits of global popular culture, in A. Scott (ed.) *The Limits of Globalization: Cases and Arguments*. London: Routledge, pp. 75–89.

Swingewood, A. (1991) *A Short History of Sociological Thought*. London: Macmillan.

Tait, G. (1993) Youth, personhood and 'practices of the self': some new directions for youth research, *Australian and New Zealand Journal of Sociology*, 29(1): 40–54, March.

Thomas, W. I. and Thomas, D. S. (1928) *The Child in America: Behavior Problems and Programs*. New York: Knopf.

Thomas, W. I. and Znaniecki, F. (1927) *The Polish Peasant in Europe and America*, vol. 2. Chicago: Chicago University Press.

Thornton, S. (1997) *Club Cultures: Music, Media and Subcultural Capital*. Cambridge: Polity.

Tinning, R. and Fitzclarence, L. (1992) Postmodern youth culture and the crisis in Australian secondary school physical education, *Quest*, 44: 287–303.

Tootelian, D. H. and Gaedeke, R. M. (1992) The teen market: An exploratory analysis of income, spending and shopping patterns, *Journal of Consumer Marketing*, 9: 35–45.

Touraine, A. (ed.) (1991) *Facing the Future: Young People and Unemployment Around the World*. Paris: United Nations.

Urry, J. (1990) *The Tourist Gaze*. London: Sage.

Veash, N. and O'Sullivan, J. (1997) Forget about Swampy. All they want is their own car, *Independent*, 19 November, p. 5.

Waters, M. (1994) *Modern Sociological Theory*. London: Sage.

Waters, M. (1995) *Globalization*. London: Routledge.

Weber, M. (1920) *The Protestant Ethic and the Spirit of Capitalism*. London: Allen and Unwin.

Weber, M. (1966) *Theory of Social and Economic Organization*. New York: Free Press (originally published in 1922).

White, M. (1993) *The Material Child: Coming of Age in America and Japan*. Oxford: Free Press.

Widdicombe, S. and Wooffitt, R. (1995) *The Language of Youth Subcultures*. London: Harvester Wheatsheaf.

Williamson, H. (1997) *Youth and Policy: Contexts and Consequences*. Aldershot: Ashgate.

Williamson, H. (1997a) Status Zer0 youth and the 'underclass': some considerations, in R. MacDonald (ed.) *Youth, the 'Underclass' and Social Exclusion*. London: Routledge, pp. 70–82.

Willis, P. (1990) *Common Culture*. Milton Keynes: Open University Press.

Wilson, E. (1992) Fashion and the postmodern body, in J. Ash and E. Wilson (eds) *Chic Thrills: A Fashion Reader*. London: Pandora, pp. 3–17.

Wood, J. (1993) Repeatable pleasures: Notes on young people's use of video, in D. Buckingham (ed.) *Reading Audiences: Young People and the Media*. Manchester: Manchester University Press, ch. 9, pp. 184–201.

Wyn, J. and White, R. (1997) *Rethinking Youth*. London: Sage.

Yardley, K. and Honess, T. (1987) *Self and Identity: Psychosocial Perspectives*. Chichester: Wiley.

Young, B. (1990) *Television Advertising and Children*. Oxford: Clarendon.

Zizek, S. (1989) *The Sublime Object of Ideology*. New York: Verso.

INDEX

